CONTENTS

03 Sophisticated online tricks of the trade 111

04 Managing success 139

Appendix 154

HOW TO USE THIS BOOK

No one doubts that the internet is the place to make money, but how can you do it for yourself, starting from scratch? This book will take you from only knowing how to switch on the computer to making so much money online that you can sell your company and buy a private plane. All the key points are illustrated by stories from business people, just like you, who have done it themselves and are honest about the problems they have faced.

Let's be realistic here: you are not going to sit down and read this book cover to cover. You want to get going! So the first three chapters have a 'quick start' section that shows you what to do if you only have 20 minutes to get going, and there are numerous 'action' bullet points to remind you what to do next. Sadly there is no quick start to finding investors, which is covered in Chapter 4 – it would be wrong to pretend that you can write a business plan in 20 minutes, but there is some good advice to follow from a successful multimillionaire.

In a worldwide recession everyone understands that selling online is potentially a fantastic opportunity: all you need is the information about what to do. This book falls into four chapters, each containing individual sections that take you from starting out to selling up and retiring! There is no need to start at the beginning: you can go straight to the chapter that interests you most and then work forward (or back) from that point.

It may be cheap to create an internet start-up, but it still requires work. To be a successful internet entrepreneur you need dedication, flexibility, 24/7 hard work and all the secrets shared in this book. Good luck!

CHAPTER 1

Starting out

In this chapter you are going to learn how to pull together the basic materials that will make your business successful online. I am going to take you step by step through the process of taking the business idea in your head into the real and immediate world of broadband communications. If you have a project that you want to start or a business that you want to expand, this is the chapter that shows you how to take the first steps. You will discover how to:

- write for websites and blogs (online diary/newsletter that will help market your ideas);
- put together your own website with an appropriate hosting company and URL;
- create marketing material including podcasts – sound or video linked to your website to explain more about your business;
- ensure your podcasts are available for everyone who wants them.

But if you need a *quick start* the first few pages of this chapter will show you how to create a simple web page. First you need to write it; then you need to get technical.

The writing

What is your big idea? The first thing to do is work out what you are going to have on your web page or the page that introduces your blog. Before you jump straight in and upload a quickly typed idea you should be aware that this is a part of the process that shouldn't be rushed. You need to devote time and thought to determine exactly how to describe your business – your web or blog opening page is the online brand that presents your ideas to the world. In other words, you need to capture the essence of your business. This is certainly not something to dash through, because it is the most crucial part of the whole exercise: everything that follows depends on it. It is worth taking time over your first description, because it will serve you over and over again in different contexts such as a more detailed website, on your weekly blog, and your sales and marketing activities through audio and video podcasts.

The content you need at this stage consists of your own company information. What you write will demonstrate why your business is moving online. If it is because you want readers to buy your product or service, you must tell them why. If you expect to find other people with similar ideas who will be interested by your blog, you must sum up your vision for the project and encourage them to follow you. If your idea is campaigning you need to explain why you feel so strongly about your cause. If you are hoping to attract a financial backer for an entrepreneurial idea, it will sum up both your vision for your project and what is driving you to make it succeed.

This is not easy. Whatever you write will probably be slightly wrong for the first version... and second... and third. Even if you are an experienced copy writer it is still bafflingly difficult to explain your business aspirations in just one page. Take a tip from professional writers who carry a note book with them and write down the ideas as they occur to them. Alternatively, talk through the idea with friends, and capture the conversation in a written note – sometimes a friend has better descriptive language, even if he or she does not fully understand your business idea. Work towards writing a couple of paragraphs. Assume that it will take at least a couple of days and maybe a couple of weeks. This is not wasted time: the longer you spend thinking about your idea the more likely you are to get it right. Print out your paragraphs and ask friends to read them for you.

There are four rules to writing your company or business information – let's call it your 'content'. These rules apply to a blog as well: learn them now and they will help you write all your digital material:

1 be accurate;

2 be straightforward;

3 keep it brief;

4 think about how it reads.

Rule 1: Be accurate

Online reputation is of great importance. If a business exaggerates the service it can provide or the quality of the goods it is selling, the users will respond and you will have negative feedback on your website. For example, if you are selling second-hand shoes, don't pretend they are new! If you are a sole trader with a consultancy business, don't suggest that you are the managing director of a large team. If you a planning to build a community of followers to your blog, you must not make mistakes. Honesty is always the best policy online. Inventing something about yourself because you hope it will help you win a job or make you appear more attractive to the people you want to reach will easily be exposed, because online everything tends to link.

Rule 2: Be straightforward

This seems easy. It's not. Write what you want to say in as few words as you can; try not to explain with lots of detail. Don't use a long word if a short one will say the same thing. Online readers are time-poor: they want to grasp your core idea in one glance.

Rule 3: Keep it brief

Imagine the different screens that your words are going to be read on. Perhaps the blog or web page will be viewed on an iPhone or a tiny portable computer; even a large monitor screen has a cut-off point. Your words need to be on one page, so keep it brief.

Rule 4: Think about how it reads

However certain you are that what you have written is perfect, there is always room for a second opinion. Ask your friends and family what they think. Better still, ask your business colleagues. If you are planning to write something every week, arrange for a friend to be available to check it for you on a weekly basis.

Check your grammar!

Although online chat has its own relaxed language, caring less about punctuation or spelling in the interests of speed, there are plenty of people who will gain a less than favourable impression if you appear to be entirely unaware of the conventions of written English. It is practically impossible to proofread what you have written yourself, so ask a friend or colleague to read through every word and check every spelling for you.

ACTION POINTS

- Don't rush your company statement – the written description of your business – everything that follows depends on it.

- Take a tip from professional writers who carry a note book with them and write down the ideas as they occur to them; this creates innovative ideas for your blog.

- The longer you spend thinking about your idea the more likely you are to get it right.

So, now you have written your first one-page text. The next step is to get technical.

Getting technical

One step at a time

If you are sole trader I suggest that you use a template to design your website to start off with. When you first set up a website, you are experimenting to see how it could work for you. Of course you want to give it a good enough shot that it won't turn out an unmitigated disaster and put you off online advertising for life – but your first website is often a case of taking the temperature of the water before you plunge right in and thoroughly immerse yourself. What you are after is a sense of how advertising online could help your business. This isn't like any other form of marketing. In traditional forms of advertising – print or broadcasting, say – costs are high, you buy your slot and you get one shot, so it is vital to get it right first time. But online you can afford to proceed step by step. You can try new things without finding yourself locked in. Getting a website up quickly, and then improving on it later, is a better and cheaper way of testing the market than spending ages mulling over different designs and trying to make your site 100 per cent perfect straight out of the gate.

Maybe you think you have spotted a gap in the market, but this is the first time you have dipped your toe, so to speak, in the business. Will it work? Are there really enough people out there who will pay the premium for your idea? If you want to see if your idea will work, consider a basic template website to see how many customers you can attract online with a trial marketing idea.

At this early stage, all you will need is a site consisting of two pages. The first is the hook to interest the customer in the product, and it will be a short description of what the product is. The second page will be the call-to-action – possibly more detail of your product, or an order form. It could contain an e-mail click-through, which will enable potential customers to contact you simply by clicking on the e-mail address to bring up a pop-up where they can write their message and send it directly to you. This, and all sorts of other possibilities, can be incorporated in your site via a template.

The homepage: your shop window

The homepage is usually the first page that visitors to your site will see, and the place they will start their journey through your products and services to a possible purchase. It is the page they reach when they type in your web address, and so it is the most important piece of the web design. It has to create a good impression and make people want to go further into the site to learn more about you and your product. If you have a larger, more complex site consisting of several pages, the homepage is not so much a doorway in as a hallway, which will contain many different doors they can enter depending on what they are looking for. One of those doorways – very probably marked 'Contact us' – should take visitors to a way of making contact, via e-mail, telephone or your postal address.

The hallway – like a hallway in a home or an office building – has to be sufficiently attractive to entice visitors in, to travel further through the site. If it feels dingy and cramped, people will back away and go elsewhere. The design and décor of that 'hallway' can say a lot about you and your business, so it is worth spending some time thinking about how to make it look attractive to your customers. Your options may be more limited if you are working from templates, but there will still be some choice. Colours can be eye-catching, but make sure they are also harmonious. Your favourite colours may be purple and green, but will they appeal to the kind of people who you want to attract as customers? Keep the text simple, and large enough to read easily – especially if you are aiming for older customers whose eyesight may not be so good.

When you have finished it, before going live with the site – 'publishing' it on the internet – show it to people you know who you trust to be honest in their responses. Being willing to listen to other people's suggestions about the look and feel of the site produces the best result. Then when you are satisfied with the initial design and content, hit the 'publish' button and wait for a response from customers.

At this point I am assuming that you are just planning a two-page website. It may just have your company information and a phone number. However simple, you are still going to need the domain name and the hosting website, but the good news is that there are many free sites that allow you to upload one page using their website template. So hurrah! At this early stage you don't need to learn HTML or hire a designer or worry about the hosting. Website templates are pre-designed websites: all you need to do is add your personal content and you're ready to jump-start your own website. Find website templates using a search tool and then upload your page to the site. You can create a one-page business listing free on Google, where you can have a simple website that you can edit any time. Compare the costs and consumer feedback of different web hosts at these addresses: **http://www.web-hosting-top.com/** and **http://uk.tophosts.com/ top25-page2.html**. You can get ranked web hosting and blog hosting companies' information on **http://rankhosting.blogspot.com/**.

Your blog

In this book I am assuming that your blog has been created for business purposes – not an online description of your daily life and shopping! Blogs began online as personal diaries kept up by the individual with regular entries. Now they are used for sharing business ideas and, of course, for marketing. When you join a blog hosting site you can link your blog back to your website, or to your LinkedIn site, or your Facebook entry. The rules for creating the front page of your blog – the purpose of your business – are the same as for creating the front page of your website.

Before you sign up as a blogger, think carefully about why you want to blog. If you are running a business that has something interesting and new to tell your customers every week or every month, then a blog is a useful method of communicating. Customers who are interested in what you have to say will also be interested in what you have to sell. Later in the book I will be showing you how to make money from your blog content.

Ask yourself:

- Have you really got something useful to tell your customers?
- Can you plan the next three months of your blogs?
- Are you an interesting writer? (Perhaps you would be better at podcasting?)

Setting up a blog is even easier than a website. The hosting sites have step by step guides, and many of them are free – **http://wordpress. com/** or Google's blog site **www.blogger.com**. Other much praised sites are Livejournal (**http://livejournal.com**), Typepad (**http://typepad. com**) and Travelpod (**www.travelpod.com**). The Posterous site (**www. posterous.com**) is perhaps the easiest to use as it allows you to e-mail your blog or send it from your phone, direct to the site, so if you can type then you can blog.

ACTION POINTS

- Work out what you want to say.
- Write it.
- Check it, and check again.
- Chose a generic template or (free) web page provider like Google.
- Upload your information.

How to put together your own website

CASE STUDY
Creating a website that keeps users coming back

Wiggly Wigglers (www.wigglywigglers.co.uk)

Heather Gorringe is passionate about ecological lifestyle and eco-gardening. She founded Wiggly Wigglers to sell worm composting kits working from her kitchen in the family farm house. As Wiggly Wigglers expanded, she has outgrown the house and now works in several of the farm's outbuildings, which she has converted for her business. Wiggly Wigglers now has a £2.5 million turnover, selling bird seed, feeders, composters, plants, flowers, turf, tools and of course the worms. Most products that she sells are sourced locally, many from her husband Phil's farm – Lower Blakemere Farm in Herefordshire in the UK.

When Heather started off Wiggly Wigglers she was totally inexperienced in business, and just wanted to 'keep going in the most wonderful part of the world'. Heather describes where she lives as having 'three times as many cows as people' so she knew she could not expect to make money selling from a farm shop. In the early days she ran a mail order company for the worm composting kits, and she advertised in national magazines, the specialist press and garden magazines. She travelled the country presenting the wormeries at garden shows and trade events.

But the business remained small and she was exhausted. 'The problem,' she said, 'is that you don't wake up one morning and say I must have a worm composting set – especially when it is easier to throw your smelly kitchen waste away. You are not going to want to bring a thousand worms into your kitchen unless you really understand why a wormery is a good idea.' The internet has been a business-changing tool because it provides information to potential customers. Heather decided that the Wiggly

Worm website should be a really useful information hub for people interested in eco-gardening, so she has packed it with specialist information about worm composting and *bokashi*, which is the Japanese composting method for kitchen waste. More important, she updates the content regularly. Her site has blogs, tweets, podcasts and Facebook groups. Heather has become famous for her Wiggly Wigglers podcasts, which draw up to 20,000 listeners per month. The site features in the generic search on Google and she uses Google AdWords to bring more customers to the site.

'I care about how people react to our information on the site. We want to attract eco-enthusiastic people to the site – we don't want lots of people who don't come back to find out more.' She tracks the people who come to the site having clicked on words that are related to 'composting' and then move to do other things in the garden such as buying wild flower seed and other ecological gardening products.

Heather remains passionate about helping people bring a positive and measurable impact to their surroundings however large or small their home or garden.

Designing your website

Building a website can cost anything from a few pounds to thousands. If you have decided to do it yourself – and there are many sites on the internet that will give you advice on how to do this – the costs are minimal. The domain name hosting company is likely to be a one-stop shop, in that it will also, for a few pounds more, lease you web space, provide you with simple templates for your web pages, and help you set up a dedicated e-mail address to go with the site. There will be tools that help you choose different designs and change the colours or the fonts, as well as enter the text. This will give you a basic, though not especially exciting, website.

If you want a website with a few more bells and whistles that is more individual, you will need to access custom web pages HTML – a process by which you go outside the template, edit the page yourself and change the look and feel more extensively. This is much more complicated than following the template system, and you will need to learn how to do it. Making it look good takes practice, and a fair eye for design.

Without a doubt, creating a website yourself is the cheapest way of doing it. But before you decide on this money-saving route, pause a moment to assess honestly your skills and abilities, as well as what you want from the website. Certainly it is not difficult to set up a basic website for yourself. But there can be a world of difference between a basic website and a good one. There is absolutely no point in spending just a few pounds to cobble together your own website if it irritates you by looking amateurish and doesn't do the job you want it to.

The alternative to building your own site is to contact one of the many small firms who do web page design for businesses. They will rapidly set you up with a professional page that contains all the right links and content that you will need to support your business. Before you choose a firm, ask a few to provide you with a list of websites they have built, and surf the internet to look at them to see if you like the style and how well they work.

A less proficient website design will drag on and wander. It will look amateurish – too many quirky typefaces on one page, backgrounds that don't enhance the foreground content, too many headings and links – a hallway with too many interconnecting doors, in which it is possible to lose yourself and never find what you are seeking. The most professional websites will feel much crisper. The imagery will be distinctive, and not have the look of a template that is used over and over again on other sites. There will be an element of real design. Visitors will know immediately that this has been professionally put together.

A great deal of thought goes into the design of a good website. It doesn't need to be all-singing, all-dancing, with videos and animation and endless pop-ups. Indeed it is often the simplest sites that work the best. Think of your site as needing to be *fit for purpose*. What does it need to have and to do to serve the basic need of your customers?

Let's imagine that you are planning a website that sells specialist walking boots for people with wide feet. You will need a website that tells your customers some information about the boots – how they are designed especially for the wider foot, possibly the different sizes and styles available, the men's version and the women's version. You will need a picture of them – several pictures, possibly, displaying them from different angles, or in different colours (supposing they come in different colours) and styles, pointing out any special features like their super-grip sole or their anatomically-shaped foot-bed. You might also consider pictures of athletic young people jumping over mountain streams wearing your boots, or posing by a dry stone wall gazing at a glorious view. Of course if you were a large company with a big budget, you could produce a clever little animation about how the bones and tendons of the foot work as a walker strides out... but that isn't necessary to sell a pair of boots to someone who has been looking for a pair that will fit.

Much more important than videos or dancing boots is the information that tells customers *how they can buy your product*. With a pair of walking boots, they might well want to try them on in a store before buying, so your website will need a list of stockists at the very least – and perhaps a link to their websites. On the other hand, if your company sells direct to the public, they might prefer to buy the boots over the telephone (where they can talk to one of your friendly sales team) or by post, or via the site itself, in which case you might want to include information not only on the mechanics of their purchase, but also on your returns policy should the boots not fit.

It is crucial to make sure that your customers can access enough information from the site to bring them to the decision to purchase, however that purchase is made.

ACTION POINTS

There is a world of difference between a basic website and a good one; pause a moment to assess honestly what you want from the website.

Make sure that your customers can access enough information from the site so they know what you are offering.

What's in a name?

One of the first things to consider when planning a website that is going to have impact with users who may be searching for your site, is your domain name. This will be part of your web address or, to give it the technical term, URL – Universal Resource Locator.

There are two possible approaches to choosing a name. You could be simply descriptive: handlebars.co.uk or bikerepairgenius.com or, if you are a chiropractor living in West Hampstead, to advertise yourself as www.westhampsteadchiropractic.net. Following on from the example above, if you are hoping to achieve success as a manufacturer or supplier of walking boots for the wide-footed, it would make obvious sense for your website address to be www.widewalkingboots.co.uk.

Many of the good names have already been taken, especially if you are in a business where there are likely to be many similar traders or practitioners. So you may have to persevere and come up with something more unusual but still, ideally, descriptive of you and your business. Heather did exactly that when she choose the Wiggly Wigglers name for her business. The more adjectives you add to the name – supremelycomfortableboots.co.uk – the more likely you are to succeed in finding a name that hasn't yet been taken. Or you might find that widewalkingboots.com has been taken, but if you use dashes creatively – widewalking-boots – you might still be able to give yourself a website address close to the original thought. Bear in mind though, that while you might poach many customers from other, similarly named sites, you could lose even more of your own who forget the dash when they type in your address.

You could take a creative approach and pick a name that is memorable that doesn't necessarily have a relevant meaning or anything at all to do with your product. Apple.com is a great example of this, and has sparked many imitators. In theory, the more obscure the name, the less likely it is to be taken – though be warned that many have trodden this path before you and however clever you think you are in picking an obscure, erudite name, someone else will already have snapped up many of the most evocative.

For small companies starting out that do not yet have a brand name, the most sensible approach is to go for the first kind of domain name – something that is helpfully descriptive of your product or service. It makes your website much easier to find, and more memorable.

Don't assume that you need to make your domain name the same as your company's name. People won't necessarily remember that it is Mark Smith and Sons who manufacture or supply supremely comfortable walking boots, but if you pick a good domain name that contains a description of your product they will still be able to find their way back to the Mark Smith and Sons website.

The place to find out what names are available, and to buy the one you want, is one of the many domain name hosting companies. If you visit one of their websites you will find the tools to check whether the name you want is available. If it is, you can then buy the right for a year or more to use that name, at a cost of only a few pounds. At the end of the year you will be asked if you want to renew the domain name. As the cost is rarely more than £8 or £10 a year, it is often worth hanging on to a good domain name even if your business using that name has temporarily gone on the back burner.

dot.co.uk or dot.com?

Both these suffixes indicate that the site is going to be primarily in English, though in theory you could build the site in any language you like. So if you choose one of these, the majority of the people who find your site will be English-speaking.

dot.com used to be the preferred suffix for businesses to pick, because it was among the first to exist (and thus suggested you had been trading on the web from the early days). However, there are now plenty of suffixes to choose from. The suffix of any website indicates different information and it is usually easy to guess what it means:

.gov – is used by governments;

.edu – used by education;

.org – shows that it is an organization (usually not for profit);

.com – the most common business address;

.co.uk, .com.au – well, you can guess the countries.

Less specifically, you might also consider dot.info and dot.net.

If someone has pipped you at the post with widewalkingboots.com, there may be nothing to stop you bagging widewalkingboots.co.uk or widewalkingboots.net. However, remember again that this could lose you as many visitors as you poach from your competitor, so what's the point? Besides, most people when choosing their domain name will at the same time buy up a number of similar ones, including most of the obvious suffixes. The expense is minimal, and it is well worth doing to save confusion between your product and someone else's site. Indeed you can buy up as many names as you want and have them all direct people to the same web page – but clearly you could waste a lot of money if you try to cover every possible permutation. It might be wiser to wait till you are a multimillion-pound global enterprise before you start buying up too many names – for the moment, focus on getting the main website name and URL up and working well.

Choosing the right host company

Domain name hosting companies do more than sell you a name. They also provide you with web space, and thus 'host' your site. So make sure you pick a reliable and reputable company when you start the process of setting up your web address.

There are plenty of tiny web hosts that come and go, but you want a bigger company with staying power and enough customers to be sure they are reputable. Choose a company that has been in business for several years at least. If possible, look for recommendations from anyone you know who has a website.

> *Most of your communications with the hosting company will be via e-mail and the web, but once you are a paying customer there may be telephone support too. The more you pay, the better technical support you will get: if you are using the least expensive version to set up a website from templates, don't expect much hand-holding.*

If you decide to change to a different domain name hosting company, you should still be able to take your domain name with you. It is much the same as switching your phone provider but keeping your number; there will usually be a small additional charge. You pay for domain names yearly and most registrars will give you a discount if you pay for multiple years.

You can be too successful!

As your website creates more traffic – more people visiting it – it may be worth thinking about spending more money on it. This is not only a question of giving it a more professional look, it's also about making sure it doesn't crash under the numbers of people trying to access it all at once. That's a good problem to have, because it should mean you're doing very good business and you can afford an upgrade!

A thousand people a day sounds a lot, and could be very exciting for your business, but most servers should be able to cope easily with those numbers. Half a million a day, and there will definitely be a problem.

ACTION POINTS

- Choose the name of your website carefully. Ideally, especially with a new company, it's worth settling on a name that is helpfully descriptive of the product or service you are offering.

- Ensure that your website offers clear and easy details of how visitors can buy your product. This is very important!

- Make sure you choose a reputable hosting company for your website.

Understanding your customers and developing your website

You know this already – of course you do – but it's such an important concept for any business today that it is worth repeating: *the internet is definitely the quickest and cheapest way to reach customers.* Why? Because the chances are that the vast majority of your potential customers are already online looking for you.

Large companies are throwing money at developing an online presence; but don't let that unnerve you. A small business can still get in with only a limited investment. It won't take long to find out what's going to work for you. You can easily control how much you want to spend, and – in case you're one jump ahead already and worrying about being swamped with too many orders too quickly for your distribution systems to handle – how many customers you want to attract.

We'll get to the hows and whats of the process in the next chapter of this book, but this is really about the why: why you or your business should have an internet presence, if you haven't already; why you need to do more than just set up a website. *You need to understand what your customers are looking for.*

Look at Google, a business that began with a simple idea – to help people find things on the internet. Now Google is not just a massive, multibillion dollar business, it is a verb. People don't search for something on the web, they Google it. The people who started Google were so successful in designing its search algorithm that it became the market leader and although competitors like Yahoo! exist, it is Google that dominates. Google is a company that understands the power of words.

That's important because with all those billions of websites already out there, and more mushrooming by the minute, the problem is to draw people to yours, rather than your competitors'. Your website is your online advertisement, but it is also essential somehow to advertise your website's existence. You will discover how to use the Google AdWords program in Chapter 2, but you probably already know that it drives more ads than anything else on the internet, and the beauty of it is that it is accessible to everybody, not just the big players with money to throw at advertising.

Let's take a look at the basics of a successful site. The very first requirement is an understanding of exactly who your customers are. It's like any business proposition: first, find out who your customers are and what they want, then provide a solution for them. This is the basic knowledge and understanding that you have to build into any product or service – and the website for it – from the start.

When you have figured out who your customers are, and their needs, and your website gives them some basic information about your product or service and your contact details, they can reach you and place an order. Once that is up and running, you can begin to drive more and more visitors to it using the targeted advertising available through Google.

The more 'niche' your product the easier this is, for the simple reason that there will be fewer other businesses in competition with you, and it will be easier to identify your customers. Let's go back to the earlier example and suppose you are the maker or supplier of wider-fitting walking boots. This is in many ways a perfect kind of product to sell via the internet, because your customers are an identifiable community (walkers) with a specific need (wider, comfortable footwear) and that need is often not catered for by ordinary high street retailers.

To draw these people to your site, rather than anyone else's, think about all the words that they might key into a search engine like Google if they are looking for your product – or indeed, to come across it by accident and then realize that it exactly fulfils a need of theirs. You might start with words like 'boots' and 'wide-fitting', or a phrase like 'wide feet'. You could be more general and think of themes like 'outdoor clothing' or 'footwear' – themes like 'fell-walking', 'moorland' or 'camping'. For any given product or service, there will be all kinds of themes that you could use to drive traffic to your site and grow your business.

It is crucial to make sure that your customers can access enough information from the site to bring them to the decision to purchase, however that will be achieved.

ACTION POINTS

- Research your competitors' domain names.

- Choose a name for your website that reflects what customers will be searching for when they want to find your product.

- Pick a domain name that contains a description of what you sell.

What's the point of podcasts?

Podcasting is a marketing tool used to help your business grow. As broadband lines have got faster, so they can carry more data. We all know that the most effective method of selling a product is not through a written document but through person-to-person contact. Podcasting is audio or video content that you create to present your business in its best light. Having read the case study earlier, if you have looked at the Wiggly Wigglers website (**wigglywigglers.co.uk**) you will see podcasts of both audio and video that sell the idea of ecological living. Instead of travelling around garden centres selling worm composting kits, the Wiggly Wigglers team have created a business that comes through the internet to the family farm.

A fast broadband connection allows you to create personalized audio and video content that can either be downloaded by your customers and watched or heard at a time that suits them, or the podcast can be viewed or heard as soon as they click on the play button. Podcasting is a new phenomenon so there are no hard and fast rules about how to do it – but there are certainly guidelines that can help you make a success of it. What I want to do is to give you enough help to start you off, then it's up to you to be creative. It doesn't matter whether you want to reach a global market or simply speak to a few dozen people.

Whether you are using audio or video, podcasting can help you establish your online identity and community. It's not difficult either. Once, mass communication was regarded as an esoteric craft, a matter for professionals. There was a kind of Brahmin class of 'experts' who were the only ones who knew how to use the specialized equipment that made broadcasting possible. But you don't have to invest thousands, or even hundreds, to make a podcast possible. You can even upload video captured on your mobile phone, though it is true that if you spend a little money, the results may be easier on the eye and the ear. Often the most successful podcasts have been those that have incorporated a clever and creative idea that has somehow captured the zeitgeist – the spirit of the times.

We'll start simple, by looking at audio (audio files, second for second, are smaller than video files). I'll show you how easy it is to devise and create your own sound podcast, recording and editing it yourself before uploading it to your website, or to a site like iTunes where it can attract new visitors to your site. Then we'll look at how to make a video podcast for use on your website and networking sites such as YouTube. All you need to start is a little imagination – and if you're stumped for ideas, the examples I'll share with you should help to set your imagination free.

Creating audio and video material

Audio

1   Write down your overall aim – what do you want to communicate?

2   If you are creating an audio podcast write the script that you will read, you will not want to speak 'off the cuff'.

3   Consider how you intend to use the podcast to get your message across. What is the story you want to tell about your business?

4   If you are planning an interview, write down what the interviewee is going to say.

5   Research your video location and think about what you plan to shoot.

6   Make contingency plans – what you will do if it rains or if your interviewee is not able to say what you expected?

7   Write down a list of all the different shots that you will have in the video.

8   Assume that with video you will record two hours to create five minutes.

CASE STUDY

Podcasting for authors and writers
**(http://www.telegraph.co.uk/culture/books/
corduroymansionsbyalexandermcca/)**

Sarah Shrubb has a wonderful job. She reads novels in the office. Of course she has to work as well because she is an Editorial Director at Little Brown publishers, where one of the most esteemed authors is the best-selling Scottish author Alexander McCall Smith. He has written over 60 books including the global best seller *No.1 Ladies' Detective Agency* series. For some time he has been serializing his stories in *The Scotsman* newspaper, so last year he decided to do the same thing with a UK national newspaper, *The Daily Telegraph*. It was very keen to publish his serialization *Corduroy Mansions* on its website. Alexander McCall Smith has another talent that makes him a natural for podcasting: he writes to be read aloud. He has perfect pacing and characters that are real to life – both heroes and villains, and all his stories have humour that makes you laugh out loud.

The UK and the United States have a tradition of serializing audio books. In the UK it extends from Radio 4's 'Book of the Week' to 'Woman's Hour'. But *Corduroy Mansions* was the first time that text and audio were simultaneously serialized in a newspaper. With 100 podcasts the reader/listener had the option to either read the text or listen: it was online in written form on *The Telegraph's* website and available via iTunes in audio form. Quite often audio editions are cut to a specific, shortened length, but because the material was podcast alongside the serialization in the newspaper, it was completely unabridged.

Sarah has considerable experience in the world of audio podcasting and thinks that for fiction the ideal length of script is between 1,000 and 1,300 words (or about 15 to 20 minutes of recorded time). She explained: 'In fiction the reader needs time to get into the character build-up and character description. You need enough of the story for it to be gripping and then build up your climax and then have a cliff-hanger. So you need at least a story in each piece. For other podcasts I think perhaps they could be a little shorter.'

The strength of the podcasts was revealed in the community-building as each podcast was launched online. People could write in and comment about the characters and say, 'This is happening, that is happening' and the author could respond.

Sarah believes that if a first-time fiction author wanted to show case work with a podcast it would be 'absolutely fine' to record the story read by the author. But a major publisher has exacting standards and the podcasts used the established actor Andrew Sachs to read the stories. She says, 'It's incredibly hard to do and you need someone who has training and skill who can come up with voices for characters and then just slip into character.'

The podcast series was a success and *Corduroy Mansion II* is to follow. What is more, the podcast did not cannibalize sales – in fact it worked as a marketing tool for the audio book, which has sold commercially.

The simplest form of podcast is a single voice conveying a story to the listener's ear. Sarah Shrubb's example can help you understand how to make *your* audio, podcast listenable, and compelling.

People respond to *stories*. A story (in words or pictures) conveys a message more effectively than anything else: you only have to think how the world's major faiths often use stories in the form of parables or myths to convey philosophical truths and religious tenets. So when you are deciding what your podcast should be, think in terms of constructing a story. It could be the story of your brand: how your company started, how that reflects your special philosophy. It might be the day-to-day story of what is happening in your organization: a kind of spoken blog. It might be the story of your product, or the story of how you were able to help one of your clients.

Sarah describes Alexander McCall Smith as a 'born storyteller', but we all have storytelling hard-wired into our brains. It's not difficult! You probably tell stories all the time, unselfconsciously, to your friends and family. 'You'll never guess what happened at work today...'.

People love listening to stories, but we are discriminating about the kind of stories that hold our attention. A good story needs to be:

- vivid;
- exciting;
- engaging;
- to the point – it shouldn't ramble.

I am often asked how long a podcast should be. The answer is: any length, provided it's the right length for the right kind of material. People say that attention spans are getting shorter, but that's probably not true. What is happening is that the things people are prepared to give their attention to have changed. If they are excited and intrigued by a clever and interesting story, they will spend longer with it. If they are bored, or simply not interested in the kind of message you are communicating, they will not be polite and wait to hear you out. They will melt away into cyberspace long before you have finished!

What is as important as length is the *shape* of the story. This is what makes it interesting and exciting. It may sound obvious to say that a good story has a beginning, a middle and an end, but that's exactly what boring storytellers forget!

The *beginning* is the hook that grabs the listeners, and makes them want to listen on. You have to catch them with the first few sentences. Compare for example: 'I have always been interested in pecuniary matters and accountancy...' to: 'It was the day my father cut off my pocket money that I decided I'd train as a financial consultant...'. The first is a description, and not a very interesting one. The second is the start of a story. Why did Dad cut off the cash? What terrible crime had our narrator committed?

The *middle* is the main body of the story. Here your job is to keep the listener interested. The story should have twists and turns, surprises and suspense, though it mustn't ramble. And finally, the story has to have a point to which it is moving – in other words, the *end.*

So – without wishing to plunge into the full technicalities of narrative theory – even the simplest form of podcast is going to take some planning. Well before you start recording, you need to ask yourself what you are trying to achieve, and how you intend to use the podcast to get your message across. What is the story you want to tell about your business?

Make some notes about your 'story' and the shape it will have before you begin writing – because you almost certainly will be writing this kind of podcast, rather than speaking off the cuff or 'ad-libbing'. As many broadcasters will tell you, unless you are a very unusual and gifted individual indeed, the best ad-libs are the ones you prepare in advance!

Finding the right words

'I can tell you what turns me off some podcasts,' says writer and broadcaster Jenni Mills. 'Long, complicated sentences, pompous, overblown language: in other words the kind of grammar and syntax that makes it impossible to follow what the podcaster is trying to get across.'

What many people fail to realize is that there is a difference between writing for the page, and writing for the ear. Jenni knows about both, because she is a novelist who teaches creative writing to MA students, but has also worked for many years in radio and television. 'Simplicity is the key,' she says. 'If the words are on a page or a screen, the reader's eye can go back over some particularly complicated thought or sentence and puzzle it out. But the ear has only one chance to grasp the meaning. If you don't make your point clearly in a podcast, the listener won't rewind. They'll switch off.'

When you have settled on what you want to say, write it in the simplest, clearest language you can. Podcasting isn't an exercise in showing off how impressive your vocabulary is, or the peerless beauty of your poetic skills! The language and grammar you use must be simple enough for listeners to grasp at first hearing. Using big words makes you sound over-keen to impress, or stiff and formal.

English is a fabulously rich language. It evolved from many roots – Norman French, Germanic Anglo-Saxon, Viking Norse, and Latin, which was the language used by churchmen and the learned, and the language of law and government in ancient times. So we often have several different words that will do pretty much the same job, though sometimes with subtle shifts in meaning – 'emancipated', 'liberated' and 'free', for instance. Basically the principle is you shouldn't use a long word when there is a shorter one that means the same thing, and you shouldn't use an elaborate one when there is a better word in more common use.

Take the words 'emaciated' and 'thin'. There is a subtle difference between them, but many people misuse 'emaciated' when the word 'thin' would do perfectly well. Unless you really mean painfully, abnormally slender, you would be better to use 'thin' in a podcast. Thin is a more everyday word. It has one syllable while emaciated has five.

To take an even simpler example: 'however', and 'but'. Both mean exactly the same thing. As a general rule, it is better to use 'but', because it's shorter and less formal, so sounds more conversational. This is not 'talking down' to your listeners. Clearly you wouldn't want them to imagine you are using words of one syllable because you believe they are not capable of understanding anything more complex. Longer words are not absolutely forbidden, but you need to use them as you would in everyday conversation.

You don't have to worry about perfect grammar. No one is going to really care if you split an infinitive and it doesn't matter if you break some of the supposed rules of written English – like starting a sentence with 'but' or 'and'.

You should avoid over-complicated sentence construction, involving lots of subordinate clauses. If you try to cram so many facts, ideas and thoughts into the sentence that you end up with an impossibly long and tottering structure, full of little asides hanging off each other like distant cousins on a particularly elaborate family tree, with a new thought here, which is meant to reinforce your main point, that is followed by a particularly striking metaphor that just occurred to you, another aside there (not to mention the odd phrase in brackets) that makes the whole thing so difficult to follow that... Um. I'm lost.

Keep it short. If it's a new thought, start a new sentence. Avoid too many 'whichs' and 'thats'. Put in a full stop instead. You are aiming for a friendly, conversational, informal style, so you also need to remember to write in contractions and apostrophes for yourself. In everyday speech, we often contract or elide words that would be kept separate in more formal writing for the page:

- 'It is' becomes 'It's'.

- 'It is not' becomes 'It isn't'.

- 'Will not' becomes 'won't'.

- 'Did not' becomes 'didn't'.

- 'I have' becomes 'I've'... and so on.

Here's an example of how *not* to do it:

> *Articulating the diverse needs of the indigenous peoples of sub-Saharan Africa is the task which the organization has set itself. Since the inception of the current strategies in 2003, the administrative body has been mindful of the underlying*

political tensions and geo-physical challenges in the region that have underpinned all the policy decisions taken by the present board, while allowing some necessary flexibility in the arrangements for the delivery and distribution of non-governmental aid, and it has been increasingly incumbent upon charities like ourselves to process the most imperative requests for assistance with reference to, effectively, a triage process.'

How about this instead? A story, told in simple words:

'Kia is 12. She's never known life free from war or famine. In her village in the Sudan, the most pressing concern is when the next lorry-load of food will arrive. Will she and her mother manage to fight their way to the front of the crowd to grab a few precious handfuls of rice and keep her baby brother alive? Helping Kia and her family is our charity's main job. We have to be ready to move the aid at a moment's notice to wherever it is most needed.'

So here in summary are the dos and don'ts of writing for podcast.

DO use:

- everyday, unpretentious vocabulary;

- short sentences;

- simple grammar;

- direct, active language;

- personalized stories.

DON'T use:

- unnecessary big words – words with one or two syllables are better than those with three or four;

- long involved sentences containing several different ideas;
- complex grammar with lots of interwoven sub-clauses – these are very difficult for the listener to follow;
- passive, impersonal language;
- abstract ideas without examples.

'People will understand you better and like you more if you use simple grammar and language,' says Jenni. 'Not only that, but you'll be glad you did when you come to record the piece. It's so much easier to voice a script if it's simply written. Fewer syllables and shorter sentences equal more breath and a stronger, more confident sound!' Talking of which....

Finding the right voice

Sarah Shrubb used an actor to bring the *Corduroy Mansions* podcast to life. Apart from the fact that Alexander McCall Smith is a busy man, on a professional production of an audio-book an actor does a different and arguably better job than the author. But there is no reason why you shouldn't be the voice of your own podcast. In fact you are probably the best person to do it! Not only do you know what you want to convey, it will come from your heart.

You don't have to have a beautiful voice, or put on a posh accent like Hyacinth Bucket (pronounced Bouquet, as she insisted) whenever she picked up the phone. All you require is confidence in what you are saying. The most important advice is to be yourself, and talk to your (invisible) listener as if he or she is just across the table from you.

'It doesn't take a special talent,' says Jenni Mills, who has trained some of the best-known broadcasters in the UK. 'The only trick is to think of yourself as explaining your thoughts to one person, rather than reading in front of an audience. When people read they often sound flat and dull. But if you can think of yourself as *talking* the piece, it will sound much more exciting and lively.'

You might find it helpful to have a friend or colleague sit opposite you while you record the podcast, so that you can talk to them and 'lift the words off the page' as the broadcasters say. Pick someone who won't make you giggle, though! The key to success is to relax and enjoy yourself while making the recording. Above all, don't worry about it. The more confident you feel, the more confident you will sound.

But what if you hate the sound of your own voice, and would rather have your teeth extracted with rusty pliers than sit in front of a microphone speaking to the world? If you really don't want to tackle the job yourself, and you have the budget, you could find a professional voice to record your podcast. Although actors can do a brilliant job, and as Sarah Shrubb says, make the best audio-book readers, for a straightforward factual podcast that doesn't need the performance element you might find a broadcaster will do as good a job, if not better. They are practised in being themselves in front of a microphone and sounding natural.

The cost of using a professional voice will vary, depending on how long the job takes and how well known the broadcaster or actor is. Experienced voice artists like Miriam Margolyes or Andrew Sachs are expensive, because you are paying for the sense of recognition and familiarity listeners will have when hearing their voice. But there may be an eager young broadcaster at your local radio station who could do the job for you much more cheaply.

Whether you are going to employ a professional voice, or tackle the job yourself, remember that it all comes back to the story you want to tell about your business. Find the right story, and the world will listen.

Video

CASE STUDY
Lauren Luke make-up tutorials
(http://www.bylaurenluke.com/looks.aspx)

Lauren Luke is a 27-year-old single mother from South Shields in the North of England who podcasts from her bedroom. She is a podcasting phenomenon. Her make-up tutorials have attracted more than 50 million hits on YouTube and, having signed up 250,000 subscribers in 70 countries, she has developed her own brand of make-up that sells online.

Lauren used to work as a taxi dispatcher where she was 'fed up with my job so I decided to start selling make-up on eBay.' At first she used a straight-forward sales technique of showing the product in a photograph, then she changed her approach: 'It's a bit boring to take photos of the product so I'd apply it to my eyes and experiment, take a photo, and then use that to show people what they could achieve.' She would use the latest colours on herself and post the results online. Within a short time the buyers started e-mailing her questions about how she applied the make-up in the photographs. The customers wanted specific product information – such as how to work with blue eyes or deep set-eyes. So Lauren decided to put video podcasts on YouTube that would show people her techniques, using the videos to link back to the postings on eBay.

At the time she had not anticipated how much the cosmetics customers were desperate to buy product from real people. Not all women feel like a super model in the product advertisements or want to be shown what to do with a product by one of those scary women in white coats who prowl the floors of grand department stores. Lauren's straightforward approach was a winner. 'I didn't expect what was to happen next; the visuals were really popular and views kept flying in – there were 100, 200, 300 saying please do celebrity looks and after school looks – it just went from strength to strength.'

So how much podcasting expertise did Lauren have? It would be fair to say, none! She began with a USB webcam plugged into her computer with the camera perched on top of the computer screen. It was cheap and she says 'the quality wasn't so good; it had a blue tinge to it'. She would check the picture on her computer before she switched to record and, because she was showing close-ups of her face she discovered that the lighting needed careful consideration. She placed a light behind the computer screen so that it shone directly on her face. She used an energy-saving bulb, and removed the lamp fitting so that the light flooded her features. She spent some time getting the lighting correct. 'I used to mess about for ages and try to get the light right and I just found that a lamp worked stuck in front of my face – I looked a bit like a ghoul but you could see the colour.' She was not worried that in the background her bedroom was clearly in shot – complete with laundry or even her dog!

Her second key element was the sound. When she started she used the microphone that was built into the computer. 'I remember it was fairly easy because I managed it, so it wouldn't have been anything too technical.'

She has upgraded her camera twice – her first upgrade was to a digital stills camera that had a video setting. She used the USB point on the computer to download the videos. Lauren's podcast are 10 minutes in length and unfortunately the camera would cut off halfway through her recording. She bought new batteries and a new memory card, but the problem continued. Recently she has upgraded a second time to a hand-held video camera and there are no problems with the length of the recording.

Occasionally Lauren would use a title at the start of the podcast and still photos at the end to show the final look, with close-ups of the eyes. She doesn't edit the material because she knows her viewers want to see what she is doing in real time: 'They want to see start to finish with no bits taken away.'

Now Lauren has her own website but she is consistent to her personal brand where customers will never feel intimidated. 'When you go shopping and you want to buy some make-up – they make you feel bad – but now I'm trying to change the beauty industry and how people perceive it. Anybody can have fun and experiment.' She always asks for feedback on every sale and she encourages people who have bought her range of make-up to make their own podcasts and show them online. 'It's something that I want to know and I can actually put it right. I don't feel you get that kind of chance with the big cosmetic companies.'

Lauren demonstrates the proof that a low-key business can be set up from a bedroom and that cosmetics do not have to be sold by super models or flawless beauties. Her videos show how to recreate make-up looks shown on TV, from 'Sex in the City' to Kylie Minogue. Podcasting from a bedroom has created a new line of make-up with worldwide sales.

Lauren Luke is a wonderful example of how to succeed with the simplest idea. You can be like her and just switch on the video camera and record what you do. But for the purposes of this chapter I am going to assume that you plan a little more. The key word here is *plan*. Before you start your video recording for your podcast you need a plan. Write down what you are trying to achieve, what your final three minutes will be like when it is an edited, finished, piece ready to upload online. Answer these questions – How long do you want it to be? What story are you telling? Who are you going to interview and what questions are you going to ask?

Planning – the shooting script

The shooting script is a list of the shots you are planning to record to tell the story. As you are both the camera person and the director of your video podcast your list needs to be detailed. Your shooting script contains:

- a list of interviewees and key points of what they are going to say;

- the location, inside and outside;

what you plan to shoot;

your contingency plans – what you will do if it is raining, people don't turn up, etc;

a list of the extra material you plan to shoot that will help tell the story.

It's impossible to have planned too much. Sort it out in your head and write it down. You can never entirely predict what's going to happen when you are shooting real people in authentic situations. Sometimes a noisy piece of machinery next door to where you're going to shoot means you have got to decamp to a totally different location. If you have written a shooting script it's much easier for you to think, 'Right, it will be okay if we go to this other location because the important things for me are listed on the shooting script and we can do that in this second location in the same way,' or, 'we can't do it exactly the same way but this is how I will alter it'. If you went there thinking, 'Oh well, I'll just kind of play it by ear' when things have changed (and they always do), your video will not tell the story you originally wanted.

Your shooting script will have listed what you want your interviews to reveal. This will help when the person you believed was a fluent interviewee becomes completely tongue-tied or has a stammer or does not say what you had planned. You have to check you script and think quickly on your feet as to how you're going to change things – 'Ok, I'm not going to interview the managing director, we are going to do the sales manager instead.' Look at your script and ask yourself, 'What were the really important things that that interviewee was going to say?' Then ask the questions to get the answers from the sales manager.

Your shooting script will contain details of the location and what you are planning to shoot. Perhaps you were planning an outside location and it is raining. Because you have written down what the overall aim is, you are not going to take lots of shots of the orchard dripping with rain and looking awful because you thought you were going there to shoot the orchard – you weren't: your aim was for a location that looked very rural, and you were using the orchard to do that. When you couldn't use the orchard to achieve that, you swopped to another thing. Your script helps you adapt when you are on location.

Finally, you will list the extra shots you will need to make the video run smoothly. Film makers call these 'cutaways' because you can edit or cut from the core material to the extra video that you have shot. Make sure you write down what you might need. For an interview you might want some material of the interviewee walking to the office, or talking on the phone. If it's essential to your story to get a good close-up, for instance, you wouldn't just shoot one and think 'Oh, that's fine I've got that.' You would need to ensure you had three different sets of pictures that you thought were good. When you get back and look at the footage on your computer, there will be at least one of them that is not as good as you thought – perhaps the interviewee moves too quickly or in the background was something you didn't notice like a plastic bag blowing about on the grass. You need to be covered for all eventualities.

Now you have finished planning you have a shooting script that lists:

- your aims and objectives;

- the interview – what will be said;

- the location – why it tells the story you want;

- the cutaways – and what they add to the story.

Framing

The first thing you need to think about when you switch the camera on is framing. The biggest mistake with video podcasting is to shoot interviews too wide. If the interviewee is too small in frame he or she cannot be seen. This is a beginner's mistake: because camera wobbles show less on a wide shot, it seems safer to use a wide frame. My advice is stay tight for a podcast: it works for Lauren Luke and her 50 million viewers – and it will work well for you!

If you're doing a short interview and you are keen to focus on what the interviewee is saying you should set up a tight shot – that is, the top of the frame being somewhere around the top of their head, cutting off the top bit of their hair, and the bottom of the frame being around about their collarbone. This, of course, does depend on how good-looking they are and how harsh the light is – but if they are reasonable looking it is a good trick for making sure that the audience concentrates on the information.

If the interview is more than a couple of minutes, it can get a bit boring so you now want to change the shot.

Changing the shot

When your interviewee is not speaking, zoom out from the tight shot. Ask a question and then add, 'Right, hold on until you answer because I'm just going to re-frame.' Then zoom out until you've got the top of their head in shot and the tops of their arms, cutting off the bottom of the frame around their chest.

The key here is to vary the interview between these two shots. You need the two shots to be appreciably different so that your eye isn't jolted when you cut between the two.

The establishing shot

At the end of your interview shoot the material that you may need to use at the start of the video. TV programme makers call this 'an establishing shot' – because you can see the person in their surroundings.

Plan your establishing shots before you shoot your interview. It's often better not to shoot them until you've actually got the interview. Most ordinary people perform better on camera if you don't make too big a deal about the process, so place the microphone on them and start going almost before they are ready. Don't make them stand there rather nervously for ages while you check the shot. Then start with two or three questions that aren't that crucial so they warm up a bit. This is a good moment to collect information you are probably not going to want in your finished interview. 'Tell me, how many years have you been in business and what's been the most difficult thing?' It's hard to listen to the content at the same time as you're thinking, 'Is my shot okay?'

When you have completed the interview, you can confidently spend more time on the establishing shots. Ask yourself, 'What does the story need to tell? Why am I using this shot?' If the story involves dairy animals, for instance, the point to get across might be, 'these animals are really well cared for,' in which case you probably want to see the interviewee walking in a field looking happy, and to have several shots of the animals, some really wide so you can see the animals grazing contentedly, and some close-ups. A good tip is to start with a big close-up where the whole screen is filled with half of the cow's head. Choose something really big and dramatic. Then cut to a wide shot of that cow chomping away, grazing in the field. Then you might have a shot of the interviewee walking along, coming to the gate, resting on the gate – then you'd cut to the interviewee in a close-up as he starts to tell you his story.

Sound in your video
The quality of your audio recording is more crucial than the quality of the video. When you're shooting video you know that it's still usable if something is slightly out of focus or the camera wobbles a bit. If viewers can't hear what is being said, you will have to start again. If you have any doubt re-read the section above on how to create the best audio for podcasts.

Placing the microphone   When you are recording an interview you need to have a separate microphone. The microphone that is fixed to the camera is not podcasting quality. It has been set up to compensate between the background noise and what someone is saying. When the speaker is quiet the background noise swells up. You will be horrified when you play back the audio and it is unusable. You need to buy a small clip-on mic, and place it close to the interviewee's head – perhaps the lapel. Make sure there is no clothing that will brush against the mic. It doesn't matter if the mic is in shot as most pod viewers feel they know the technology of recording and will not be surprised to see it.

Lighting

An expensive camera with an expensive lens will handle the contrast between bright and shady light. A less expensive camera will have problems. If you are shooting a head and shoulders with bright sky behind them, or with a white wall that is reflecting a great deal of light, it will create a contrast. On a cheap camera the contrast will make the head and face seem very dark. To the naked eye there will be no contrast because your eye is better at compensating than a camera lens. So, the best light for videoing an interview is when it's a bit cloudy with soft overall light.

Indoor versus outdoor   Modern cameras are excellent at recording using indoor light. However, don't shoot your interviewee up against a window as the contrast between the outdoor daylight and the indoor light will be too strong and you will have the dark head problem. You should be able to shoot most situations with natural light without having to 'light' it yourself.

If you have a reading light or a spot light you can bounce the light off a white wall onto someone's face: bounced light tends to be flattering. Don't shine the light directly at the interviewee as it will make them squint. Look around the room and choose your inter- viewee's position carefully. The professionals' trick is to backlight.

Out of shot, have an angle poise lamp shine some light directly onto the back of the head creating a halo effect around the hair so that the interviewee stands out from the background.

Cutaway shots

A cutaway shot enables you to edit your material. Imagine that you ask three questions and you want to use the first question and the third one but the second answer was boring. You will you want to cut it out. You can just chop the first and third ones together, but it looks jumpy. So you would want to put a cutaway shot in the middle to hide where you are editing.

The aim of the cutaway is to create a bridge between the two shots. It enables you to tell the story without clunking jumps that hit the viewer in the eye. Of course there is a more informal style of shooting where the viewer is used to jumpy sequences and the camera moving around, or where the camera swoops as if you were standing there and looking. However, cutaways can solve technical hitches in the edit, so make sure you shoot lots of material.

Cutaways can solve the problem of changes in contrast. If you've got a dull day and suddenly the sun comes out and changes the contrast, the video will look too bright. If you're shooting a big movie, you put down your tools until the sun goes back in and start again when it is shady. If you don't have time to waste, shoot a cutaway at the moment the light moves from cloudy to bright sun and bright sun to cloudy so that you could accommodate those changes.

Using the tripod

Sometimes, the interviewer wants to appear in the finished video as well as ask the questions. Now you have a choice – either get somebody else to shoot for you, or put the camera on a tripod and frame the shot so that you are both in full view. The downside of the tripod is that you have a static shot. If your interview is longer than a minute and a half, stop and change the shot to a close-up of the interviewee. The upside is that the tripod keeps the camera completely steady, but this in turn can be a problem. When you put together material that's been shot on a tripod with footage from a hand-held camera the material looks uncomfortable. Try and stick with hand-held shooting. It feels more immediate and informal.

Make-up

Ordinary day make-up is fine for most podcasts; any heavy make-up will ruin the authenticity of the participants. If your podcast is important to your business, you want to be believable, credible and authentic in order to genuinely impart the information. Lauren has proved to all podcasters that natural is a good look. But, remember that the camera notices light more than a human eye. If light is bouncing off a shiny bald head, it will dominate the shot. Instead of listening to the important things being said, the viewer will be distracted by the shine. So, carry a little loose face powder and the problem is solved.

Props

There is a simple rule for props: if you need one prop, take several spares as well. Imagine you plan to shoot a scene of a girl feeding a horse an apple – you need more than one apple. By the time the microphone has fallen off, you forgot to remove the lens cap, and you didn't manage to get the apple in shot, or the sun went in, that greedy horse will have eaten four or five apples. You need enough props for several takes.

Interviewing

Don't ask the same question twice. Assuming your interviewee is not an actor or a professional speaker, you will discover that most people are very rarely better on 'take two' than they were on 'take one'. Most people take two or three questions to warm up when you are using a video to record them, so save your important question until they have been talking for a minute or two. Listen carefully to the reply and make sure that it's not waffling on too much. Waffle is difficult to edit. My advice is to carry on, and then ask the same key question in a slightly different way. Your interviewee might say, 'But you've already asked me' and you just say, 'Tell me again.' If you say, 'Stop, your first explanation was too long – try and tell me in a shorter way' your interviewee may becomes self-conscious and then continue in an unnatural style.

De-clutter

In the case study Lauren chose not to de-clutter her bedroom and has made a feature of the normal everyday parts of her life that appear on camera. She is deliberately showing the beauty world her normal cluttered life. However, if you are planning a different story you need to hold in your mind the idea that all the things that make somewhere look better to the naked eye work well on camera. If you de-clutter before you shoot it is easier to notice what you have got in the background. It's easy to ignore something in shot until you return to the edit and see that the cable from your camera is snaking around on the carpet. It hits you in the eye when you are editing on your computer but you didn't notice it at the time. Look carefully at all the different parts of your shot on your screen – use the viewfinder and then look again without it.

Ratio of recording to edited material

If you were making a professional television programme you might well expect to create four to five minutes of factual programme in an eight-hour day. For a podcast you will be trying to avoid feeling over-rehearsed and lacking spontaneity. To be authentic you might need to move quickly, so assume at minimum a couple of hours, but first check out these common mistakes.

Length   If your podcast is explaining something, try to be concise. Most people ramble when they speak. It seems fine when you are recording, and then when you are editing it you'll be cursing yourself for everything being too long. The biggest difference between professionally produced material and amateurs 'having a go' is length. If you are the producer it is easy to over-estimate the interest of your audience and how long their attention span is going to last.

A good rule of thumb is that specialist information will command a longer attention span. For example, a teenage girl passionate about ponies will watch an information video on a website about horse riding for 20 minutes – what is more she will concentrate and look at how they are riding. Compare that to an advertisement on the television where the entire story is told in 30 seconds. Don't be self-indulgent. Don't draw things out too much.

Curse of the boss   If you're the managing director of a company you might think you've got something really important to tell your staff in your podcast – think what you've got to say. Say it to yourself and then ruthlessly make yourself say it in half the time. I suppose if the staff are paid to listen, you can keep going all day, but if you want your staff to be interested and entertained, be snappy. If it's a message that is going to be seen by clients, remember they won't be prepared to be bored.

If you're producing a video podcast for the MD, don't invite the sack by saying, 'Look, you're being boring, do it quicker.' Instead, try saying, 'That was marvellous, fantastic, brilliant – now just go over that again, but we've got to be really concise. This time let's just try and get point A and point B across and forget everything else.'

Most viewers have a short attention span – when you've had the problems that the edit suite throws up, you'll be sitting there thinking, 'Why didn't I do that again?' 'Why didn't I do that shorter?'

Written piece to camera   If you are determined to read as you face the camera, it had better be interesting! It is better to appear as if you're just talking to people directly, as Lauren does in her make-up podcasts. Even if you stumble a bit or don't get your words exactly right it's nearly always more interesting than reading. If you have some important figures that you need to read aloud, you will need to top and tail the reading with a section where you are just looking into the camera and speaking to people off the cuff.

Shifty eyes – look into the camera   Look 'down the lens' – if you look slightly off you look shifty and untrustworthy. If you pin up a script beside the camera and your eyes are sliding across and refocusing slightly when you read, you will look untrustworthy. Try and sit still. The most common nightmare is to have someone on a swivel chair moving from side to side as they talk. You barely notice when you are in the room and you're interviewing, but the camera picks it up. Editing, you will be kicking yourself and saying, 'Why didn't I tell him not to swivel his chair?' 'Why didn't I make him stay still; how could I not have noticed that?' The camera picks up mannerisms more than the human eye.

Slow pans   Panning shots (where you are moving the camera sideways or up and down) are nearly always too slow. Imagine you had a cottage for rental. You wanted to show that the cottage was near the sea – so you shoot the sea and then you pan across onto the cottage – it takes 20 seconds. That's too long. It's boring when you're watching it on screen. Keep doing the same shot again and again, each one faster than before. When you've done one that is so fast that you think, 'That's far too fast, nobody will be able to tell what's happening' you will have the shot you will use in the edit.

One-shot action   If you have a very steady hand you could try and shoot all the action without stopping. It's much harder than you think to do one shot that has lots of different action. For example, you might need to walk towards the person who is talking, and if you wobble the camera the video will look as if you are in an earthquake! If you are filming animals or children they will move around; you could try and follow them, but they can quickly move out of your shot and then you have to start the video sequence again.

It is great fun to try, but hard to pull off – especially if you want to do something that depends on separate bits of action all happening within the same shot. It takes time, careful planning, and a team who can remain natural doing the same thing again and again.

Use of zoom   Avoid zooming in unless for comic effect or you want a 'crash zoom' from one object to another. You are almost always better off without zooming.

ACTION POINTS

- Have a plan.
- Include plans for the interview, location and cutaways.
- The quality of the audio is more important than the pictures.
- Use a tight shot.
- Don't ask the same question twice.
- Don't record too much.

How to edit audio

CASE STUDY   *The Economist*

The Economist is an authoritative weekly news magazine focusing on international politics and business news, edited in London and published on glossy paper. It has a growing circulation of about 1.6 million copies selling internationally. As well as world news, politics and business, *The Economist* covers books and arts, science and technology and publishes regular in-depth special reports including *Technology Quarterly*. The editorial is aimed at highly educated readers and it claims an audience of opinion formers and policy-makers.

But *The Economist* had a problem. It was a good problem, but it needed a solution. Like all magazines and newspapers, *The Economist* found that subscribers cited 'no time to read' in their top three reasons for subscription cancellation. Readers of *The Economist* are busy executives and are time poor. If you have ever taken a weekly subscription, it's easy to find a pile of magazines that you've read part of but never completed. *The Economist*'s digital strategy was very forward thinking in recognizing that offering an alternative digital platform in audio was complementary to both its online and print content. If you subscribe to the magazine you have access to the audio and you can listen to the sections you choose on your iPod or MP3 player as you drive to work, or when you are out on a run. The audio podcasting is not a substitute for the print, but it augments the experience. The digital technology of podcasting allows for a weekly audio version of the magazine for people who are time poor but information hungry.

The Economist audio version is created by Jennifer Howard, MD of Talking Issues. She says that:

> *The majority of podcast listeners for* The Economist *come from the US, followed by Asia and Europe, and they say they listen to it in their car, on the train and in the gym, and they are getting through*

far more of the magazine than they would ever have time to read.
A lot of people have said 'thank god for the audio edition, I would
have cancelled my subscription otherwise'.

Jennifer's company records between six-and-a-half to eight hours every week. She has a simple process. She records, which she says 'is the easy part', then she edits and then she has what she calls a 'proof listen' to ensure the material is accurate. With an international audience she knows that the pronunciation of names has to be perfect – and with 21 languages in any one week it's easy to make mistakes. If she's unable to track down the correct pronunciation of a personal name for example, at the very least Talking Issues ensures that the pronunciation across the article is consistent. The next step is a fine edit and then the audio is converted to both MP3 and M4a format at 48 kbps. Before the material is uploaded, Jennifer will tag the metadata with the article name, the selection name, the article number, and attach any artwork. Finally she'll code each podcast with the copyright details so that when it appears in the iTunes library or MP3 libraries the copyright is in place and the audio articles appear in the same order as the print edition.

Some weeks she is dealing with as many as 90 MP3 files in one zip folder and one six-and-a-half-hour M4a file. Then it is easy for the user to either download the one MP3 folder, or subscribe to an RSS feed which pushes the M4a file to the listener's iTunes library. Jennifer thinks it's important that the audio users can browse the material in exactly the same way as you browse a magazine.

Because Jennifer is creating six or seven hours every week she has considerable experience in how to record the material in the easiest and quickest way. It's her job to make sure that the audio version is ready to be downloaded before the print version is on the news-stands or delivered to the home of the subscriber. She says, 'What we do is practically live; we're reading printed material and recording it with as few mistakes as possible so that we have a one-and-a-half to one ratio when we edit.' Jennifer's advice is to create a paper edit as the recording is happening. She has the script in front of her and marks the place where there's a problem and an edit is needed. She says there are always problems. 'Tummy rumbles, script rustles, exclamations, coughing, not to mention stumbling over the international names!' She's convinced it's worth every effort to ensure the audio is as clear as possible, because quality is important to the user.

'Content and production quality is key to a good podcast. Nobody wants to listen to somebody recording in their bathroom.' Her results are professional and *The Economist* is downloaded by more than 60,000 people each week.

The first rule of editing is to back up every copy of the digital recording. As you work on the edit make sure you're creating back-ups of your podcast – you never know when you might have a power cut or computer virus.

The second exciting element of sound editing is that it's a visual as well as an audio skill. Sound editing equipment produces graphic representation of the sound waves, so you can see what you are editing, and some equipment will remove background noise and interference with one click.

Excellent editing

The characteristics of a great editor are easy to identify but hard to find; spoken word editors are a rarity except in top recording studios or working at the BBC. Often the best sound editors are musicians because they have an excellent ear for cadence and pace; although they must be interested in speech and the spoken word. If your podcast is a disposable product, today's news and of no interest in a week, you'll be considering an edit ratio of 2:1. For something that aims to be the quality of an audio-book, however, the ratio is more like 3:1 or more. When editing, in both cases you need to listen for mistakes and the loudest noises. Most podcasts will leave in minor little clicks or breathing because that's part of reality.

As a sound editor the most important area for you to concentrate on is clarity. Does what's being said make any sense? The sound editor will be listening for inflection, cadence and pace in the voice, all of which should help make the recording clear to the listener. If you're going to have to pronounce tricky words then consistency is a key skill. When you've decided how to pronounce a word, then stick with that pronunciation for the complete podcast. Nobody gets the words correct every time and with a podcast you have a global audience that will e-mail you and tell you you haven't correctly pronounced the first name of the President of Azerbaijan! In the meanwhile, like Jennifer, as editor you will be cutting out any extraneous noises, breath, clicks.

Digital technology makes it simple to record material on your computer and share audio files with friends. You can record the material you require and then before creating a file to upload you can remove any noises you don't want. With the graphics of the sound on display you can see where to add the sound or make the edit. So you can synchronize music with speech or import new material and add it to your edit. If you're self-producing, my advice is to have a couple of goes at recording the entire podcast without stopping and then take the best version. If there's something that was missed in the recording session you may need a re-take.

Don't worry if you make a mistake, it's easy to stumble on a word you think you know well, such as 'immeasurably'. It looks simple to say, but is easy to stutter over. Sometimes words just hit you, you just can't get past them and it's worth knowing there are good reasons why you'll have problems. Two consecutive vowels, or a long word that starts with a vowel, can disturb even the most professional actor. If you find you need three or four takes, use the beginning of take one up to the place where the audio is 'fluffed' and then use the best correct take following the fluff. So you might cut across from the middle of the sentence when you patch in the re-takes. If your original recording was at an unusual location with a noisy background, make sure you've recorded some 'atmosphere' as a background audio that you can use as background or space filler on difficult sound edits.

Cover up your mistakes

There's no question that it takes a while to learn to sound edit, but the basic concept is straightforward: take out what you don't like and cover up any other mistakes. Music creates atmosphere and can run under the recorded sound. If you need to hide a difficult edit you can increase the volume and that will distract the pod listener. Don't get carried away though with the power of music as your audience is really interested in hearing what you have to say. Music is an effect and should be balanced with the dialogue. Music creates punctuation to speech, it can be used to introduce different interviews or different emotions. More often it's used as an introduction and conclusion to each podcast. Sound effects are fun to add but it's a classic beginner's mistake to use excessive sound effects. You'll recognize a beginner's audio by the use of echo, reverb, and vibro effects. Don't show off, just concentrate on the story you're trying to tell. Sound effects can be a distraction from the words; ask a friend or colleague to give an honest opinion whether they work or not.

Sound effects

Background effects are a less obvious editor's trick. They create mood and sense of place. Take your microphone to a range of different places and start recording your own background library. The beach in summer with seagulls shrieking and children laughing and the sound of waves breaking on the sand, or the shake and rattle of an approaching underground train. Most useful is the sound of the office; murmurs from meetings, the tip tap of the keyboard, the quiet ring of the phone. Of course you can buy CD's of sound effects, but recordings from your own business will be more convincing.

Editing equipment

Some editing software is available free. Free software is not just free of cost, as in 'free drinks'. It's free as in freedom, like 'free speech'. Free software gives you the freedom to use a program, study how it works, improve it and share it with others. This free software is also called 'open source software', because the source code is available for anyone to study or use. There are thousands of free and open source programs, including the Firefox web browser, the OpenOffice.org office suite and entire Linux-based operating systems such as Ubuntu. For more information, visit the Free Software Foundation.

An example of free software is Audacity, which was developed by a group of volunteers and distributed under the GNU General Public License (GPL). It's an easy-to-use audio editor and recorder for Windows, Mac OS X, GNU/Linux and other operating systems. You can use Audacity to:

- record live audio;

- convert tapes and records into digital recordings or CDs;

- edit Ogg Vorbis, MP3, WAV or AIFF sound files;

- cut, copy, splice or mix sounds together;

- change the speed or pitch of a recording.

Then there are sound editing packages that are free at a basic level but the manufacturers are convinced that when you start to use them you'll want to upgrade to a better level and they'll charge you for the additional effects and features.

An example of the free but you'll have to buy to upgrade is the WavePad Sound Editor audio editing software for PC & Windows, Mac OS X or Pocket PC. It claims its easy to use interface means you'll be able to start editing in just a few minutes. It allows you to record and edit music, voice and other audio recordings. When editing audio files you can cut, copy and paste parts of recordings then add effects like echo, amplification and noise reduction. The manufacturer's aim is that you'll want to upgrade and purchase a WavePad Master's Edition with audio restoration features including enhanced noise reduction and click pop removal.

There are also professional sound editing packages from international brands such as Sony and Phillips that are on sale at a medium price and claim they provide a complete professional digital audio production suite.

For those of you for whom the music on the podcast is going to be an important element of the pod experience then music orientated software such as the ProTools system has advanced music creation and production software and many new virtual instruments and plug-ins for music. If you're concentrating on talk then SADiE provides the tools for serious voice pod production and was created by experienced recording engineers. The SADiE sales spiel is that it can be used on location, even in a mobile truck, as well as in the office, for multi-track editing, mixing, working to picture or in CD mastering. You will be surprised to hear that SADiE claims to have the slickest, fastest and most user-friendly interface!

If you browse the many different sound packages available on the market you'll see that many of them are without particular distinguishing features. You can buy them online. Then you download them or upload them onto your own laptop and you go from there. How long it takes to learn to use them depends on how good your technical skills are. You should be able to pick it up in a morning, longer if you're resistant to technology. It's not complicated, though.

Top tips for audio editing

- Back up every copy of the digital recording.

- Your aim is to achieve clarity.

- Listen for mistakes and the loudest noises. Leave minor problems in.

- Take your microphone to a range of different places and start recording your own background library.

- Buy an editing package with a free tutorial.

ACTION POINTS

- Do not start editing your audio before you have created a back-up. Digital audio back-ups are as simple to create as a saved copy of a Word document. Unfortunately simple things are easy to forget. Create the back-up and label it with the time and date. Then if you have any problems with your edit you can return to the original file.

How to edit your podcast

CASE STUDY
Ben Brownlee – Curious Turtle Editing

Ben Brownlee has been an editor for over a decade. He runs his own business, Curious Turtle, from his home in Denmark. Primarily a training company offering courses in the most popular video editing applications, Curious Turtle also accepts editing contracts from a range of clients, both for broadcast and for the web.

Ben has found that web-based projects, whether viral advertising snippets, video podcasts or corporate identity promotional videos, have been on an upward curve for a while:

> *The advent of faster broadband connections has meant that more and more companies are incorporating video into their web presence. It's now possible to present genuinely good quality video on the web, which hasn't been the case until relatively recently.*

Faster internet access allows Ben to perform his editing remotely and costs have been significantly lowered, with no need for expensive shipping of tapes back and forth. 'Client approval videos are sent by e-mail, changes are returned by e-mail and the final edit is delivered either completely digitally onto an ftp site or mastered onto a DVD.'

Yet while faster access, greater bandwidth and an increasingly computer-literate world have all helped Curious Turtle to flourish, familiar problems continue to surface associated with the editing process:

> *As an editor, I'm often not involved in the early stages of a project. Someone else has planned and shot the material and it's my job to shape it into something that tells the client's story and that shows their business in a positive light. The material I receive has often been shot by someone without a great deal of experience. Too much footage is a common problem in such cases, but, while time-consuming, it doesn't hinder the editing process as much as not shooting the right kind of material.*

Ben recently edited a four-minute video for an architectural firm with the aim of providing a corporate profile made up of shots of their offices, details of some of their projects and standard to-camera interviews. It was a simple project aimed at bringing their architectural achievements to life without relying on pages of text and standard still images. Unfortunately, Ben's task turned out to be far from simple.

The first issue concerned the location of the interviews. Recorded in the offices themselves, scant attention had been paid to the setting and the background was full of clutter and office paraphernalia. Ben remembers:

> It was far too distracting There were too many elements in the shot that simply did not belong in a nice, sleek presentation. On top of that, the camera was static at all times, which meant it was difficult to make a clean edit when trying, for example, to match the beginning of one sentence with the end of another.

To remedy the situation, Ben took advantage of a fundamental difference between creating video for the web and for television:

> The size of the picture for the web is small, so it's possible to crop footage without sacrificing the quality of the image itself. It's not a perfect solution, but in this case I used a cropping and scaling technique to remove much of the background to ensure that the viewer's focus remained on the interviewee.

> The cropping also served a second purpose of allowing me to create the illusion of camera movement. When I cut between different sections of a particular interview, the edit did not jar with the viewer because I was able to cut from a wider shot to what appeared to be a close-up. It improved the flow and made it appear more dynamic than a long, static interview, despite the content being essentially the same.

A second problem was an irritating hum from a microphone that plagued the entire recording:

> There are a few different ways of dealing with sound issues, but on this occasion I employed a noise reduction technique. Basically, the software analyses a sample of the hum and is then able to

> *return to the footage and reduce those frequencies. Although it*
> *may not eliminate the hum completely, it can drastically improve*
> *the quality of the sound.*

Finally, Ben was left with a more delicate concern. The main interviewees had all been asked to think carefully about what they wanted to say and to distil it into small chunks where possible. The reason was two-fold. Because of the immediate nature of the internet and the ability everyone has of navigating away from a page with a single click, it's vital to grab attention and get a message across without boring the viewer. Secondly, and especially if it's a video that might be watched by a large number of people, there are issues surrounding server costs. Long videos usually result in a poorer quality of image.

Even so, several of the interviewees spoke for over 25 minutes each. While Ben knew there were ways of cutting the interviews down effectively, he had to guard against potentially causing offence to those who were, after all, paying for his services.

His solution involved some clever diplomacy:

> *What I did was to present them with two final versions. The first*
> *was, to be blunt, something approaching a wall of sound with the*
> *interviewees talking for far too long.*
>
> *The second was a similar edit offering the same message,*
> *except I had removed the material that I felt was redundant.*
>
> *I was able to lead them towards the shorter, more concise version*
> *that I knew would work far better for the web, but the choice was*
> *still theirs.*

Ben allowed his clients to become part of the editing process and to feel like they had made the decision to reduce their personal content for the good of the video overall:

In the end, what it comes down to is either making a shorter video that looks better or making a longer video with a lower image quality because it needs more compression. What we arrived at together was a sharp, clean, fresh piece of material that the client was happy with, which is really the most important thing!

In this section I'll explain how it's possible for anyone to edit their own video podcast cheaply and to a good standard. As with any technology, it's possible to spend extra money to produce ever more impressive pieces of work, but cost need not be a factor and previous editing experience is not a prerequisite for creating an attractive, effective video for your website.

Getting started – software

Most home computers manufactured in the last few years are capable of editing video with no problems at all. In fact, PCs and Macs usually come with free editing software, Windows Movie Maker and iMovie, respectively. If you don't have either of these programmes you can download them from the web, but feel free to browse other no-fee alternatives such as Jump Cut, Jahshaka or VideoSpin.

Programmes such as Movie Maker and iMovie make it easy to transfer material from a standard DV camera to your computer. From there you can make basic edits to produce your video and export it to a format suitable for playing online, or onto a DVD that you can pass around to friends or clients.

These programs are specifically designed for people without editing experience, so if you have made a careful plan of your shoot and have a clear idea of what you want to achieve, then they are perfectly adequate tools for creating a decent standard of content.

Naturally, free software is limited in comparison with more professional programs. Really fine editing is not possible, so be prepared for the fact that you'll be more reliant on longer shots rather than MTV-style fast-paced cuts. This isn't necessarily a drawback, though, especially if you're just starting out. The temptation to indulge in all the flashy aspects of a more complicated editing program can have a detrimental effect on any project.

Free software wouldn't have been sufficient to produce the kind of sleek, professional video Ben Brownlee delivered to the architectural firm in our case study. The limitations regarding the number of cuts and the quality of edits, along with a reduced freedom to use music and alter the audio, would have made his task impossible. Yet basic software doesn't have to result in an inferior video. If you consider how to convey your message in the simplest way, without relying on fancy editing techniques, you can create a video that would look at home on the most modern of websites. This kind of software may not be perfect, but it allows you to import images and graphics and its very simplicity will force you to focus on sharp, absorbing content.

Upgrading your software

If you believe that your project needs more precise editing than free software can offer, or perhaps having shot and edited a few successful video podcasts of your own you feel you are ready to move to the next level, then there are a variety of programs you can purchase. They won't guarantee that your video will be better than one produced by free software, but they will open up new doors and offer you the chance to raise your ambitions.

For Windows, a popular solution is Adobe Premier while for the Mac a decent place to start is Final Cut Express. Be aware that these and similar products are not something you can grab and intuitively pick up in a few minutes, but at the same time there are manuals and online tutorials that can help you. Many companies, such as Curious Turtle, offer more intensive courses and inexpensive DVD training programs that can have you up and running within a few hours.

The decision on whether to invest in this software comes down to the kind of video you want to produce and the amount of time you can commit to your project. If it's fairly uncomplicated, perhaps using interviews, graphics and some music, it's perfectly possible for anyone to learn how to use such software with relative ease. If you want to go further, to immerse yourself in the craft of editing, then it's worth considering professional instruction.

Selecting your material

Once you've shot your material and feel you're capable with whatever editing software you've decided to use, you're ready to start shaping your video. In fact, thinking of the editing process as crafting a sculpture is a useful metaphor.

The first thing to do is select the 'stones' you want to use. At this stage you're searching for the basic building blocks of your sculpture. Start by watching the footage and when you think you've seen something useful, transfer it from your camera to your computer, giving yourself plenty of leeway either side of the section. There's a definite balance to be struck here; don't limit your choices by rejecting too much material, but at the same time don't confuse yourself by transferring too much and wasting disk space at the same time.

Keep in mind how long you expect the final video to last and use it as a reference point. Of course, much depends on how much material is available, but, as we saw with Ben's project, you could be faced with a couple of hours of footage that needs to be whittled down to a mere four minutes. In a case like that, this rough pre-edit should see you eliminate an hour or more of the material.

Shaping your material

The second stage is to begin shaping the outline of your sculpture, to start forming the broad basis of the story you're trying to tell. Whether it's for a feature film, a 30-minute comedy or a four-minute promotional video, you're always telling a story. It sounds almost too simple, but start looking for your beginning, middle and end. Remember you want to create an engaging video, not just a random collection of scenes or interviews. Poor editing can make even brilliant footage look tame, but in contrast, clever, vibrant editing can render the most mundane subjects interesting.

Work quickly here. Watch the footage, drop the sections you like into your timeline and move on. This is one of the most creative moments of the process so don't get waylaid by details; just keep those creative juices flowing. Don't worry too much about how it looks and feels at this stage, all you're looking for is an overall shape.

Applying the detail

If we imagine that your final video is aimed at being four minutes long, you should now be left with about eight or nine minutes of material. Before you do anything else, watch what you have and you'll notice that some sections will seem too long and others will seem out of place or redundant. Having established the shape of your sculpture, it's time to use your finer tools to craft some detail.

You may find that sections that seemed perfect now appear out of place. Be brave and remove them or relocate them to another part of your story. Remember that nothing is locked down; you can always reinstate pieces of footage later if you wish.

To craft your final version you'll now start to smooth over your edits by utilizing cutaways, or covering shots, to improve the flow. If we return to the Curious Turtle example, Ben shrank large amounts of interview footage down to just a few minutes while still maintaining the course of the story. When you reach this stage, a good tip is to concentrate on the sound rather than the pictures. Pick up the three or four sentences that you want to link together to make your point and place them together on your timeline. You'll be left with a sound-track that makes sense, although the pictures will be jumpy and untidy.

For his video, Ben used a range of cutaways to cover these edits, including images of architecture and general office footage. Your cutaways will depend on your subject, but the important thing is to remember your story. Keep the cutaways relevant to what the interviewee is talking about and make sure they reflect where your story is heading. Cutaways can be as simple as a gesticulating hand that emphasises a point or a carefully placed image that illustrates the product or service being discussed.

The finished product

When you believe your video is near completion, stop work altogether and take a break. If you can sleep on it then so much the better, but if you are pressed for time then walk away for at least half an hour.

Editing is an intensive process and it can be easy to become blind to any potential problems. A proper break will create some distance between yourself and the video and give you fresh eyes next time you look at it. When you return to the material you will need to be critical of your own work and be ruthless enough to remove any section that isn't contributing properly to the overall piece.

Think about what you're trying to achieve with your video podcast. If you're marketing a new product, have you explained why your product is better than or different from everything else on the market? Have you kept faith with your original objective? Make sure everything in your video genuinely enhances the progression of the story.

This isn't about equipment; it's about content. There are many videos online that have long, boring sections that drag on without having a point, or videos that are full of dead air and dead space. Keep yours concise and compact because it's so easy for people to click away to a competitor who's more adept at holding their attention.

There's a law of diminishing returns when it comes to honing and attempting to perfect your video, so draw a line and stop or you'll drive yourself mad. Show it to a friend. Question them about it. Is the message clear? Did any section feel too long? Would they have liked more information about a certain aspect?

Editing is an intensely personal process and objectivity can be difficult to achieve, but while it's important to consider all criticism, don't abandon your ego altogether. If you really believe in something you must fight for it, just be sure you know why.

Common problems and how to deal with them

Buzzing or humming on the soundtrack

In our case study, Ben dealt with a faulty microphone by using a noise reduction filter. This is undoubtedly an effective method that's possible with more advanced editing suites, but there are other ways of fixing sound problems.

First, any kind of speech often forces more mundane noises into the background because viewers are listening to what's being said. That means a buzz is often only an issue when no one's talking. In this case, simply turn the sound down for a few seconds between speeches and the buzz will 'miraculously' seem to disappear.

Second, a continuous music soundtrack can divert a viewer's attention from any possible hum. The use of music could have a separate beneficial effect of craftily shielding a slightly dodgy edit as well. The art of cutting is about not jolting the viewer and continuous music helps to smooth the passage.

Uncomfortable interviewees

It's extremely obvious to any viewer when an interviewee feels uncomfortable in front of the camera. Even if the words make perfect sense the viewer may be distracted by darting eyes or fidgety hands and the message can easily be lost.

If you're faced with such a dilemma then you need to utilize your cutaways. Take a brief moment to establish who is talking and then try to cover their discomfort by using their speech as narration over other footage or images. Always be sure to follow their thought processes though, and make sure your cutaways are relevant to what's being said.

Remembering your medium

Always keep in mind that people will not be viewing your video podcast on their 40-inch widescreen HD TV. There are numerous examples online where this has been forgotten and as a result shots are too wide and the main subject too small. If you are faced with this problem, try Ben's method of cropping the image to place the subject firmly in the foreground.

It might be fun to make lots of flashy cuts and try to create an MTV-style effect to your video, but for the web this isn't very effective. Because of the limitations of final compressions, changing shots every second really only means that the picture quality of your video will be reduced. Rein in your wildest ambitions. Higher quality can be achieved through greater simplicity.

Another common problem with online videos is a lack of focus. If you can make your point in three minutes, do it. Your seven-minute version may look prettier, but people will grow bored and tune out if they're not receiving new information.

Don't make edits just for the sake of it. Have a browse online and you'll come across videos that cut with metronomic precision every four seconds for no discernible reason. The effect of this can be hypnotic and the rhythm becomes boring, so mix up your edits, keep it interesting and make sure every edit has a point.

Special effects

It may be tempting, but keep your fingers away from those special effects. As much as they may seem fun and new to you, the fact is that everyone has seen most special effects before and you run the risk of producing an amateurish piece of work.

A grammar of editing has been built up over many years. If you're determined to use an unusual transition, make sure it has a point, such as using a clock-wipe to indicate a passage of time. Ninety-five per cent of your edits will be straightforward cuts or cross-fades, ideal for a transition to a new location or subject, and if you keep that in mind you shouldn't go too far wrong.

Top tips for video editing

- Free software may have limitations, but use this as a positive to create a simple but effective video.

- Plan the story you want to tell in advance and always keep it in mind.

- When beginning the edit, don't get bogged down in small details.

- Keep your cutaways relevant and ensure they reflect the story you want to tell.

- When you think you have finished, take a break.

- You'll return to your work with fresh objectivity.

- Ask a friend to give their thoughts on your video.

- Don't be too ambitious. Simplicity and clarity is key to a successful online video.

- Make sure every edit has a point.

QUESTION

Before you start your edit, do you know how long you want the final video to last?

ACTION POINTS

- Your final video podcast will depend on how much material is useful. If you are a beginner you will probably have shot much more material than you can use – so decide how long the podcast is going to be and then create a 'rough cut' which may not be perfect but will help you eliminate material and save time in the editing process.

How to upload your podcast

Now you need to activate your podcast. This section will show you how to upload content that is audio or video so that you can create a compelling website for your customers:

- add your material to the free podcast sites such as the iTunes website;

- work out if you have enough storage space on your own site to hold your material;

- understand 'the bandwidth' figure – the size of the podcast files multiplied by the number of people who will be downloading it at any one time.

Quick uploading

Uploading to specialist podcast sites (free)

If you have followed the advice earlier in this chapter you will have created some compelling material that is either valuable in its own right, or is an excellent marketing tool for your business. But what are you going to do with it? Perhaps the best known podcast site is iTunes, but there are also many others. Type 'podcast hosting' into your search engine and you will get the most up to date list. Use the one that is most appropriate for your content. These companies will not only store you podcasts (so you do not have to own a website) but also will give you information about how many people have downloaded it. If you want to link to the podcast from your website you will need to create a link from your site to the podcast. So, you need to make sure that you have given your podcast a proper label (known as 'meta-data') that tells everyone what it contains, so it can be searched for and found among other similar material. Pretty simple....

Before you hit the publish button just make sure your podcast has:

- a name or title;

- an episode number and description;

- the link to your MP3 file (that's the digital audio encoding format that compresses the sound) so that it plays back on digital audio players;

- any other key words that will help Google or other search engines find your podcast.

How to add your podcast to the iTunes website

1   Open the iTunes program.

2   Sign in to the iTunes Store and your account. (If you do not have an iTunes account, click on the button on the top right that reads 'Sign in'. Create your account and make sure you are logged in.)

3   Within the Store, click on the Podcasts section, which brings you to the podcast directory.

4   Click 'Submit a Podcast'.

5   Enter your podcast feed URL (do this by copy and paste so you don't make a mistake).

6   Click 'Continue' and iTunes will offer a new screen for you to fill in with information to tag the podcast (for example the language it is recorded in, what category it falls under).

7   Click both 'Confirm' and 'Submit' and wait for the e-mail saying your podcast has been accepted.

Rather slower uploading

If you already have your own website and URL, and it is the place you want to put your podcast, you need to work out if you have enough storage space to hold it and, just as important, if you have enough space for users to come to the site and download the podcast.

Return to your hosting company and check that it has room for the audio podcast (most hosting companies allow for one gigabyte of storage). If you are planning a series of podcasts this is the moment to work out how much space they are going to take up on your site. Ask yourself:

- What length is each MP3 audio file?

- Is the file 42 kilobits or 129 kbps per second?

- How many episodes am I planning?

- How many episodes will I have available at any one time?

A simple rule of thumb is to multiply the answer to the first question (the length in minutes) by the size of the file (42 or 129) to find out how big your files are going to be, and then by the number of episodes to find out how much storage you need.

Now you need to work out if lots of people are going to download at the same time. Here you need to know what is called 'the bandwidth' figure – the size of the podcast files multiplied by the number of people who will be downloading them at any one time. Of course, you won't know until you have started podcasting. Make a guess and tell your hosting company; you can always increase the hosting space at a later date.

Really Simple Syndication (RSS)

You will also want to create an RSS feed so that your users can have an automatic checking system that lets them know you have updated the site. RRS feeds are useful for all updating – blog entries, news headlines, audio and video – and use a standardized format. Your website users will tell the RSS reader that they want to receive your updated podcasts; the podcast is sent to them and can be read using software called an 'RSS reader'. Your podcast users will have the RSS reader either on their desktop computer or on their mobile. They subscribe to your service by entering into the reader your URL or by clicking an RSS icon in a browser.

RSS feeds are available free; the free feeds are fine for someone who is not doing lots of podcasts. However, they will not give you subscriber and download statistics. If you are slightly more ambitious you can set up a 'pay as you go' account with other hosting companies that will charge by how much you upload each month and give you the RSS feed for free. If you are considerably more ambitious you are looking for your own web server and will probably need an IT professional to help you set it up.

ACTION POINTS

- Convert the file to MP3 format – conversion technology is available free online.

- If things go wrong, check the file size.

- Work out 'the bandwidth' figure – the size of the podcast files multiplied by the number of people who will be downloading it at any one time.

- Create an RSS feed, available free.

CASE STUDY

Uploading technology (http://www.talkingissues.com/home)

This is the story of Jennifer Howard and her company Talking Issues, which successfully records and edits podcasts for *The Economist*. She has a great personality and when she talks about her successful business she makes it sound trouble-free. However, her company almost went out of business when her server crashed and she was told that the cost of new technology was more than she could possibly afford.

When Jennifer set up the Talking Issues website for the audio versions of *The Economist*, she discussed her requirements with the computer team who cabled her offices. They agreed to set up a computer server for the podcasts. The computer team needed clear information on how many downloads of *The Economist* would take place each week. Jennifer didn't know. It was a new service; it might be popular, but then again how could she be certain how many people would download the podcast?

She considered for a while, and with help from the management team at *The Economist* replied, 'Let's assume we are going to get 50,000 downloads a week.' So, her computer team set up a server and space from a network in East London, and the service went live. In the first week *The Economist* had 12,000 downloads; in week two the numbers had increased to about 15,000. In week three the server crashed – not because she had more than the 50,000 downloads she had specified (in fact she had 60,000, which the server could handle) – but because she had 60,000 concurrent downloads.

The Economist is not a service where people occasionally throughout the week download the audio. Readers want to hear the audio the very moment it is available. So, when *The Economist* readers in New York get out of bed in the morning and go online, they download the podcast. Then readers in Chicago go online and start their downloads. Then Los Angeles comes online and then Buenos Aires and on it goes around the globe – huge numbers of people all downloading at the same time and crashing the server with requests. Jennifer had four days to sort out the crisis before the following week's edition went live on the site.

She asked her friendly local company to create a solution. 'They did a lot of teeth sucking and heavy sighing. Then they specced us a whole rack of servers. Their plan was that as more people came online around the world, a new server was available. Unfortunately that was going to cost us £900,000. Literally, we might as well have shut the doors right then. Our business was finished before we had started.' Jennifer desperately needed an alternative.

Fortunately another IT expert suggested an international cache system. Now Jennifer uses a company called Cache Fly. This is a content delivery network provider that relies on routing the material rather than holding it in a fixed place. So if you are in Chicago, the material diverts to the Chicago server. If you are in Paris it diverts to the Paris server. It eliminates waiting time and rather than 'hosting' the material, the system focuses on delivering.

The lesson learnt from her story is that the host or server on which you are placing your podcast needs to be sufficient to your users needs. You need to plan ahead.

The whole point of creating a podcast is so that other people can listen to it on their mobile or on their computer while at their desk. Most mobiles support MP3 and MP4 files, so that is what you are going to be creating for your users.

File format

When you have made your recording you will have created your podcast as a digital Wav file, which is saved at 705 kilobits per second. You can put this Wav file directly onto a disc or CD or keep it on your computer. To make the file suitable to go on your website or onto iTunes to be downloaded you will need to convert the file to MP3 format, and before you upload your podcast you need to convert it to a smaller size of 48 bits per second. You are going to squash the file and remove some of the audio detail to make it quicker to upload and download. All the bits above and below the recorded level will be compressed and squashed. For voice quality there is not a noticeable difference – usually only sound engineers can identify a compressed voice audio. However with music (which has a broader aspect) you don't want to squash the sound and compress the top and bottom notes, so if you are going to podcast music you might want to consider using a larger file size.

For the moment let's stay with your mainly speech-based audio or video recording. I will assume that you have completed the editing and checked that the sound levels are at a good quality throughout. There are two technical terms to know: render and convert.

Rendering: first you need to render all the different tracks into one final piece. Your Wav file is made up of the different tracks and when rendered they will be pushed into one track, which is a mix of every-thing you have added to the podcast.

Converting: then your audio needs to be converted from the Wav into a squashed podcast file that is easy to upload and download. Here you have choice as to the size of the file: 42 kilobits per second is the quickest to download but not the best in terms of sound quality; 128 kbps is preferable but will be slower. At present most users will be familiar with the MP3 files, but the latest technology is an MP4 A file, which uses less space, is quicker to download and is higher quality. It is not difficult to predict that it will overtake MP3 in the future and is probably the way to go if you want to future-proof your business.

Converting is easier than you might think

Conversion software is simple to use. You open the software and a window appears. Drag the Wav file into the window. Choose the folder where you would like the converted file to end up and then click 'Convert'. Your MP3 file is in the folder ready to upload.

The good news is that you can find free conversion tools online. The Switch Sound file converter is easy to master, and there are many others available. However, you might want to consider buying conversion technology. If you do so, you will get technical back-up support: warranties and training that will help should things go wrong. If you have spent hours creating your podcast you don't want to lose the file!

Sometimes there are problems converting; here are some fixes:

- Check the file is where you left it (maybe it has been removed).

- Check the file is not corrupt preventing the converter from recognizing the coding.

- Check the file size – if the conversion fails it is likely that your file size is too large for the free software you are using. You might need to sign up for a more sophisticated converter.

CHAPTER 2

How to use your website to sell online

In this chapter you are going to learn how to use your website and blogs to sell products and services online. I am going to take you step by step through the simple process of creating advertisements that will bring people to your website, using Google AdWords. Then I will show your different methods of selling, so even if you plan to keep your product in your spare bedroom or garage, you can start straight away. You will discover:

- how you need to understand your customers in order to develop your website and how it is described;

- how to set up advertisements using Google AdWords;

- how to make your advertisements relevant and have them clicked on;

- different methods of selling online.

But if you need a *quick start* the first few pages of this chapter will show you how to:

set up your AdWords Account;

prepare your web page ready for your buyers to visit;

make sure you don't spend too much money;

write an ad and understand how to choose a keyword;

write more ads using the 'Create Another Ad' function.

CASE STUDY
Holiday Home Rental (**http://www.holidayhome.ca/**)

This is a case study of a man who is time-poor, but had a problem to solve. His name is Robin and he is the owner of a mountain cabin in the Canadian Rockies. Robin is time-poor because he is a city broker in Calgary, Alberta and his weekends and evenings are spent mountain climbing or skiing in the Rockies. He is not interested in spending his precious leisure time sitting at home in front of a computer, and he uses Google AdWords so that he has more time to spend trekking in the wilderness.

Five years ago Robin decided to rent out his cabin in the Rockies at the times when he was not using it himself. He knew there was no point in hanging a 'to rent' notice on the door of the cabin because it is not close to a main road, but is up a long track in the middle of nowhere. So, he prepared a printed brochure and gave it to the tourist office in his nearest small town – Golden, British Colombia. Nothing happened. No one rented.

Then Robin spent a week of late nights, after work in the city, building his own website – putting up pictures of the cabin and describing how it has four bedrooms and great views of the mountains. He could have used a web designer, but he enjoyed doing it himself. At the same time he paid $100 Canadian to a home rentals website that listed his cabin as a holiday rental. He told me, 'The companies that work as a compendium of individual owners have "three month free listing" introductory offers on their websites, so I posted my site details on several other rental sites.'

This was a smart idea because links to other websites help lift your website listing in the organic or non-sponsored part of the Google search engine. But that was not enough to create website traffic to his site and help him rent out the cabin.

When Robin returned from one of his many mountain trips, he registered with Google AdWords. Then he sat round with some climbing friends and a few beers and made a list of all the AdWords that would attract rental interest in the cabin. He says, 'It was an animated discussion and we listed lots of ideas. We thought of all the words holiday makers might search for – ski holiday homes, cabin home, mountain biking cabin, British Colombia cabins, Golden vacations, and many other iterations.'

The great thing about Google AdWords is that it is very simple. Robin realized that he should drop any words that did not work and within a few days realized that 'all of them were useless'. Of course he did not have to pay for the words that were no good, because no one clicked on them.

Over the following months Robin experimented with more words to discover the three keywords to bring visitors to his website and ensure that his cabin is now full with paying visitors all the year round. He said, 'I pay for three words – Golden BC and Golden British Colombia – which gives me 600 hits a month. I know there is lots of complexity of the AdWords that could have been used, but I'm not interested. I don't want to bother.'

Robin has continued to use the same three keywords and just one advertisement that hasn't changed. 'Golden BC Vacation Home' is his headline; 'Spectacular private 4-bedroom house in the Rocky Mountains, **www.holidayhome.ca**' is the ad wording.

Today 85 per cent of his bookings come from the internet and the remainder from word of mouth and return guests. Interestingly, when Robin started using AdWords none of his competitors were advertising online. He admits, 'I've only got 15 or 20 real vacation home competitors and then the hotels or lodges in the Golden area, and five years ago when I started doing this nobody had heard of AdWords. But now that has changed. What has happened is that the competition for the words "Golden BC" has increased – I started off paying 7 cents a click and now it has increased to 25 cents a click and I am one of the bottom listed advertisements on the search – so maybe the top guys are paying as much 50 cents or even a dollar per click.'

About once every couple of months Robin goes to Google.com/analytics. He clicks 'Access' and enters his password to find more information about the people who visit the website. 'I have set my budget to 30 bucks a month, and get about 20 visitors a day. Some days are busier – for some reason Tuesdays are busiest for people looking for holidays. I can see that the average time spent on the site is a minute; and they look at 5.3 pages. Google tells me that 90 per cent are new visits and there is a great map that shows me where the visitors come from – the majority are from Canada and the USA and this month there were two from Italy and five from the UK. And looking at my customers who actually book, the ratio is the same – 80 per cent Canadian, 10 per cent American and 5 per cent from Europe.' Robin believes that the traditional holiday booking agencies are going out of work, and there is a whole new business of individuals using Google AdWords to rent their own properties.

Robin thinks that if you are time-poor there is no need to go further: 'I could spend more time on second or third best keywords and play with them, but I can't be bothered; my paying clients just go to my website and e-mail me or call me and that's fine with me. The cabin is good and full – 90 per cent full during peak tourist times, and just a few days empty when schedules don't fit. And it's full every weekend during the year. It's as good as it gets.'

If you can use a laptop in bed, there is no need to get out from under the duvet – and you don't need to be a nerd to get started on Google AdWords. In less than half an hour you are going to be an internet advertising executive with new customers visiting your website, but first you need to set up a Google AdWords account and the next few pages will show you how to do it. Your aim is to make sure that your advertisement for your product is one of the top 10 advertisements when a potential customer runs a Google search.

Setting up your AdWords account

First, type '**www.adwords.Google.com**' into your browser, and choose 'Try AdWords now'.

The first sentence you see offers help with creating your own website. Now click on 'Starter Edition' and then click 'Continue' at the bottom of the screen. The first section is called 'Location and Language'. Choose United Kingdom, or the country where your business is based and then let's assume you are going to do everything in English.

In the 'Write your Ad' section enter the address of your website main page (some people call this the landing page, as you want your customers to land on it). This address is your URL.

Now, go back to the start and check this again. It is really easy to make mistakes when you are working online. You need to check location and language and, most important, ensure that you have typed in your web address correctly – you don't want to send people to someone else's website.

Congratulations, you are close to having an account!

Now let's write the AdWords copy. This is the creative bit. Enter the headline to describe 'my product' and complete the two lines of text to add further information. The headline can contain no more than 25 characters, while the two descriptive lines can contain up to 35 characters each.

Are you a words person or a numbers person? Some people find this writing part easy, but then have problems looking at the data and numbers that explain the success of the ad. If you are a numbers person don't worry. Click the link: 'The five keys to powerful ads' for advice from Google about writing an effective ad. Go for it. Try and get your first draft down now and you can improve it later. This is not like traditional advertising where you have to get the words perfect first time. You will make more money if you are flexible – be prepared to change what you write as your skills develop.

Now you are ready to think of keywords that describe your new product. Think of just one – the most obvious word is best. Write it in the text box. Put square brackets [ ] around the keyword. There is more about this later, but for now just get going and choose your first keyword.

Choose the currency that you are going to pay with, and set yourself a low monthly budget – start with the sum that it would take you to buy a pair of shoes and then you can test if this works for you. In some territories Google suggests you start with a minimum figure.

Click 'Continue' to go to your account and then you have a choice: if you already have an account with Google (perhaps for gmail or spreadsheets or other Google applications) you could use the same account settings, or you can create a new account. Enter your password twice and your e-mail address. Read the terms and privacy policy. The next page will tell you to check your e-mail to verify your account. The e-mail you have been sent from AdWords will have an account number. Write it down and keep it somewhere safe with your password. Click 'Continue'.

Well done! You now have a Google AdWords Account.

You are going to organize your account in three simple steps. You have already completed step one – setting up the account. Then you plan the campaigns, then ad groups that contain keywords and ads. Now make sure that your two-page site contains a description of what you plan to sell, and your e-mail address and phone number so your clients can contact you from the first page (go back to Chapter 1 for more on this). Think of it like a postcard in the newsagent's window – but in this case you are not dependent on everyone walking by the shop. You have the entire internet at your fingertips and no one need know you are still under the duvet.

Go back to adwords.Google.com, click the 'Try AdWords now' button and this time select the 'Help me create a website with Google Sites' link. Google will help you set up your own site and register your domain name.

You will have to enter your name and address and phone and e-mail address in the text boxes. The page will allow you to select a Google map of your location – this can be very useful if you are selling a product that is location-specific, for example if you are a beauty salon your customers will want to see where you are based. You can also choose a Google phone number that will forward the calls to you – the good thing about this item is that Google will count the phone calls for you.

Now you have started building the website, you will start thinking about all the extra features you want – pictures, discussion pages, audio, video and more – but there is one key thing you must never forget: the purpose of your site is to attract traffic.

Attracting traffic

Whiz-bang features do not create traffic. You have placed a needle in a haystack. People certainly aren't going to just stumble upon your site by accident and it's unrealistic to believe that a good idea is all you need.

No one is going to find your site unless you tell people about it, and online it is not about word of mouth, but about search engine appeal, so your site must appeal to the search engines. People will then visit your site because they have found it in a search. Later on you can add the user interactivity that will make your site more appealing to customers, but now you must concentrate on the AdWords that will help the search engines find your website.

If that's too complicated and you want to get going straight away, click on the 'I don't have a web page button'. Google allows you to choose your location and the hours you want the web page to be shown. (This is very useful if you are time-poor like Robin and can only talk to the people who want to rent the cabin in the evening on his home phone number when he is back from the city. If you are going to place your office phone number on the page you might want to take the page down at certain times of the day – perhaps when you are collecting your children from school and are not available to answer the phone.)

Make sure that your web page copy describes what you do (show it to a friend and ask their opinion). Google allows you to upload pictures and choose a background colour for your page. When you have finished, click 'continue' and your URL for your web page will be a Google address, such as myproduct.Googlepages.com.

Now that your website is up and running let's go back to the keywords you chose when you set up your account. First type your keyword into the Google search engine and find out who your top 10 competitors are. You will see their ads on the right hand side of the screen, and sometimes the top ones are across the top of the page. If you want to know how many competitors there are, keep scrolling down the pages until you see the number one ad repeated. The total number is the number of people who want to use that keyword.

Remember the brackets you put around the keyword? That ensures that the search will only be for that exact word. You will want to type in lots of different words. That comes later. Start with one, or maybe two. If you change your mind about the keyword you have chosen, click 'Delete' next to the keyword and it will be removed.

When you write the keyword into the square bracket you are asking AdWords to find you an exact match against the keyword. Try to think of the square brackets as something that creates a bucket around the word. Later in the book I'll show you how to put lots of other words into your bucket.

Setting your budget

Remember your monthly ad budget? You set it at the price of a pair of shoes a month. Now you have a decision to make – how much are you prepared to spend each day? If you have only a small budget then it is better to be at the bottom of the top 10 ads that are viewed by everyone all the time, than to spend it all at once by being at the top for a shorter length of time.

If you are feeling adventurous, Google has a Budget Optimizer that will give you the largest number of clicks possible for the monthly budget you have identified. You can set this for yourself by clicking on 'Edit Settings' in the Control Panel and next to 'Bidding' uncheck the 'Budget Optimizer' – write in the amount you want to spend and hit the 'Save' button. You can go in very low and see where you ad is placed, or try for the highest sum. On the other hand, if you want to play safe the Google Budget Optimizer will give you the average value for your market.

As this your first foray into AdWords you do not want to be the number one – not only is it the highest price, but also you are likely to have people who don't want to buy anything clicking through to your site. Every click is something you will have to pay for. You want clicks from real buyers.

Be competitive with yourself

Have a further look at the ad you wrote 10 minutes ago – could you do better? Have another go: write a second ad and go back to your ad group and upload it. In the control panel page click the 'Create Another Ad' button and on the next page choose the 'Variation On My Current Ad' option. When you have written it, click the 'Create ad' button. This new ad will be used as an alternative to the first. Which is going to be more successful? Google will automatically test out your new ad and if it is more effective then Google will show it more often; the system chooses the top ads for you. How many ads can you have at one time? Up to 50! So get writing.

Being competitive with yourself is called 'split testing' – it is a useful marketing tool that helps you identify what kind of ad will reach your customers. You can try using ads that are only slightly different and see which one works best for you.

Get to know your control panel

When you have set up your account you will notice a Google alert at the top of the page. You can close it if you are too busy – or read the frequently asked questions that arrive with the new account details. When the amount of money you have placed is about to run out, Google will use the alert to contact you.

Your ad will appear on your control panel looking exactly the same as it will in the search results. Click on it to make sure that you have entered the page address accurately. It is very easy to get this wrong, and you don't want to send potential customers to the wrong page or even the wrong website. If you have typed in the wrong URL address, return to AdWords and click on the 'Edit' button to fix the problem. Don't forget to save your work.

The control panel shows the links that will provide the analysis your business needs to measure your AdWords success. Click on these links to find out more:

Keywords – these are the two words you have chosen so far.

Impressions – that is the number of times your ad has been displayed as a result of a search.

Clicks – that is the individual visitor numbers clicking on your ad and arriving on your website landing page.

Total cost – this is the cost per click multiplied by the number of clicks.

When you have clicked on one of the links, information will be shown to you in a column of figures with the highest numbers at the top. This is the place where the numbers experts come into their own. They may not have been happy writing the ad, but they are going to love looking at these figures. There is a 'Graphs' button for you to click on the right of the screen and you can print out your graphs in Microsoft Excel. If you click on the keyword link again the column will swap to ascending order. This information will show you which key-words are getting the most impressions and you can start to think about how your business is performing in the marketplace.

ACTION POINTS

- Type a word that describes your business into the Google search engine and find out who your top 10 competitors are.

- Choose 'Try AdWords' now.

- Click on the 'I don't have a web page' button to set up a web page.

- Make sure that your web page copy describes what you do and has your e-mail correct.

- Set a small monthly budget.

- Remember you do not want to be the number one – not only is it the highest price, but also you are likely to have people who don't want to buy anything clicking through to your site.

- Be confident – it doesn't matter if you get this wrong. Every time you log into Google you can tweak your advertisement or change your keywords.

- Get to know your control panel.

How to set up advertisements using Google AdWords

It doesn't take a genius to work out that the quickest and cheapest way to sell yourself or your business these days is via the internet. If you have a product or service that needs marketing, a website can put you in touch with thousands of new customers at the click of a mouse button.

But it isn't enough simply to have a web presence. How will people be drawn to your site out of the billions they could access? Here are some statistics to ponder: 100,000 new websites are built daily, and 125,000 people start a home-based business every week. So it follows that you need to find some way to make your site and your business cut through the abundance of others.

You need to advertise your product or service, or yourself, using the latest internet-based tools. It is easy, but there are many pitfalls. Reading this chapter will show you how to save time and money.

Before you start using the Google search engine as a tool for advertising your product or service let me just explain why it's important to your business:

- AdWords perform between two and 10 times better than other advertising.

- When someone is actively searching for something like a new car they're already in the mood to buy.

- Information about your customers will help you make sales.

CASE STUDY
Selling a commodity product that
everyone uses – light bulbs (**www.enviro-lights.co.uk**)

Liam Darch-Wood's story begins with a problem in the kitchen. He is a very keen cook and likes to try Italian-inspired food that he prepares for his wife Vikki, and then left-overs are gobbled up by his lovely cocker spaniel, Fudge. The problem is not the cooking, but the light bulbs in the kitchen. He told me, 'We have a lighting rack with four MR16 spotlights on; they seem to go all the time and I would hazard a guess at around 14 or 15 a year. I think it might be grease from the cooking that makes them blow. I used to have to physically take the blown bulb to B&Q to get exactly what I wanted and you can only buy them in packs of two.'

Liam's search for light bulbs was the inspiration for his website Enviro-lights. co.uk where he offers savings by buying light bulbs in packs of four, 10 and 20. Liam understands retail because he left school halfway through his A levels to work for Morrison's supermarkets. He became the store's youngest ever department manager at 20 and his store in Derby was also in the top 10 in terms of turnover. But his real business interest is in search engine sales, and Enviro-lights.co.uk is part of his company TDW Commerce that he plans will become an empire of e-commerce stores, all driven by search engines. Enviro-lights.co.uk is the first product of this project, with Caravan & Camping equipment the next in the pipeline. Liam is convinced that Google AdWords creates an entirely new business model of retailing based on the Google search engine.

Liam is sympathetic to the problems of the traditional retailers. 'If you open a shop you have to pay rent on the space and you have to stock the whole shop with every single item.' As a customer after light bulbs for his kitchen he walked round the DIY stores looking at their racks and racks of light bulbs feeling frustrated that the bulb he was looking for was not available. He says, 'In a shop you can't display every item and therefore a customer will think you don't actually sell it and there are literally tens of thousands of different bulbs that you can buy. You probably buy a light fitting and you never really know what bulb goes in it until you've got it home and realized that you can't get bulbs for it.' So Liam's site specializes in the more difficult to obtain bulbs such as those needed for security lights or decorative lighting. Liam knows his customers suddenly discover they need a specialist bulb.

When he began the business Liam set a clear advertising budget of the price of a pair of shoes a day and has been happy with the return. He has used AdWords to advertise one section of lighting at a time, starting with halogen lights. This allowed the business to keep customers focused in one area, and build up stock in that particular section before moving to a new lighting area. The company uses AdWords to build knowledge of the customer and stock at the same time.

How do you describe a light bulb? It is more difficult than you might at first think. For example, a very small halogen capsule light bulb caused him problems. Liam described how on the box and in the catalogue the light was described as 'capsule' and he assumed that would be the word customers would use in their online search. He was wrong. He used many different varieties of how people might describe the bulb, waited a week and then analysed the data. 'We tried "halogen capsule" or "halogen capsules", "capsule lamps", "capsule lamp", and there was not a lot of traffic for something that should be selling quite well, so then we tried describing the light by the name of the fitting – "G4 bulbs" and "G4 halogen bulbs" and immediately the traffic patterns changed dramatically.' At this point Liam rewrote his advert, so instead of saying 'We sell halogen capsules', it said 'We sell G4 bulbs'. What Liam discovered was that to sell the capsule light bulb he needed Google AdWords of 'G4 bulb' or 'G4 halogen bulb'.

Liam's other key learning is the importance of uniformity between the keyword searched for, the advert delivered, and what is viewed on the website. When he discovered that G4 halogen bulbs and G4 bulbs were the two most popular search words, he made sure that the advert contained that particular key phrase. When customers go through to the landing page of the website the key phrase is also prominent.

Liam uses conversion tracking that shows when a sale has been triggered by a particular advert or keyword. Through the conversion tracking he assesses which of the landing pages has been most effective over a period of time. Conversion tracking is a very simple piece of code that Liam has placed on the website page that says, 'Thank you for your order' and, 'Your order has been successful' – these are the pages of his website that mean that a sale has taken place. 'So as soon as somebody gets to that page, it triggers the code, and Google can track back to what keyword and which advert it was that they clicked on.'

He did this using the 'Conversion Tracking' button on the website and clicking on 'is this a sale or an enquiry or a lead'. He said, 'You literally press a button and it generates a code for you – five lines of java script – I sent it to my web developer and he just popped it in the page.' It only takes a couple of minutes to put up and only needs to be done once. Now Liam can see how many clicks he has had and the cost per conversion all on one screen. Your conversion code is available within your AdWords account, under the tools section. If you have access to your website html, you copy and paste the code into your html, just above the closing </body> tag towards the end of the page.

So what was the most difficult part in setting up the business? Nothing to do with the AdWords! It was packaging: 'The most difficult thing for me was just the logistics of posting out a light bulb and how I would deal with that, not how I was going to get the business out there.'

Liam understood the importance of matching the keyword searched for, the advert delivered, and what is viewed on his website. You will need to do the same if your customers are likely to use search engines to find your website. Search engines decide whether a page is relevant – the most appropriate one to meet the search you're typing in – by how many other people link to it. It's a simple premise: if your website has a lot of people linking to it from other web pages it's pretty likely that it has good stuff on it. If other people are telling the world that they think your page is worth reading by putting a link on their page to yours, it's a good way of measuring how useful the information on the page might be.

Search engines work on what is called 'PageRank', which evaluates the quality and appropriateness of any web page based on how many other people link to it. PageRank is an algorithm – a mathematical process which, following a search, determines which page shows up first, second, third and so on. It's completely automated so there are no humans involved in the ranking mechanism.

On a Google search results page there are typically 10 ads on the right-hand side of the page headed 'Sponsored Links' (sometimes also along the top of the page). Naturally, the lower your ad is down that page, the less likely it is to be clicked, and if you are 11th and on the second page then you might as well be wearing an invisibility cloak. But don't worry: by reading this book you'll find out exactly how to keep your ad right near the top of the list.

The main improvement is that the position of your ad is based not just on how much you pay, but also on how well your ad performs. If you have an ad that's very relevant and performs very, very well Google will give you a boost in your ranking for the same amount of money. As you know from Liam's experience, the ad that is more appealing is the one that fits what is being searched for and gets clicked on more often and will get an advantage.

The reason why AdWords are so effective compared to other advertising (they perform between two and 10 times better) is that when someone is actively searching for something like a new car they're already in the mood to buy. If you can put a relevant ad in front of that person then you're much more likely to make a sale.

Google spotted that the search was a very strong indication of desire to purchase and that advertisements can fulfil the need of the searcher. All other advertising media – newspapers, magazines, television – are mass market. Everybody will see a television ad for light bulbs whether they are looking to buy one or not. If you are an advertiser you are wasting money on the 99.99 per cent of people who aren't in the market for light bulbs. However, if you advertise on Google the only people who will see your ad for light bulbs are those who are actually interested in purchasing, which means more effective advertising with greater efficiency.

You might get closer to your purchaser if you advertise your light bulbs in a home improvements magazine or on a TV channel showing home makeover shows, but again those readers or viewers aren't necessarily looking to buy light bulbs (especially as many readers and viewers don't actually do any home improvements – they just find the programme relaxing or fancy the presenter). Most of the audience probably already have the light bulbs that they want or perhaps they are simply not in the mood to buy when they are browsing a magazine or watching television. Working with topic-specific media is good, but it's still not the same as an internet search when someone is actively looking. It's the 'active' versus 'passive' that makes the difference. The person doing a search is leaning forward, not sitting back.

If you're actively searching for a light bulb for your new and unusual light fitting your behaviour is going to be different from when you're browsing a magazine and happen to see a halogen bulb ad. Searching for a product online is especially effective if you have a clear idea of what you want because the advertisements are going to be targeted directly towards your needs.

Google's massive computing power gives it a genuine advantage over competitors because it can search, analyse the AdWords and reveal the results at such a tremendous speed.

Google's customer orientation

Google's motto is 'don't do evil'. Unlike the auction of advertisements, which favours companies with more money and is aimed at quickly generating a lot of income for the search provider, Google wants to make sure that people can find the information they are looking for as easily as possible and to provide the best possible experience for all the people who use its website.

The ads that Google runs alongside the search results are rated on how well they perform. If the ad is not performing well – meaning it's not being clicked on – it probably means it's not very relevant to the search that person was doing, and Google will correspondingly drop the ad down the page and finally stop showing it. In this way, your experience of searching online for halogen bulbs will be better because if someone has written a poor or irrelevant ad, Google won't even show it to you. It wants to make your search experience as helpful as possible.

It may be making billions of dollars, but Google is still very customer-oriented. In fact, you might even say that it is making billions *because* it focuses on the customer. By reading this book and being customer-oriented yourself, you can make money as well.

Google now has an 80 per cent market share of online advertising, but there are other search engines you might consider, such as Bing, Yahoo!, Facebook or LinkedIn. There are different methods for building your ads in each and there are differences, for example, on how many words you are allowed to use in your ad.

Google's market capitalization is now over $100 billion with more than $20 billion annual revenue, and it is still growing. So we know that AdWords really works. So how do you make it work for you? It's really easy. Anybody can do it. To use Google AdWords you don't have to work for a top advertising agency. You can do it at home and there is no big mystery to it. I am going to show you how!

ACTION POINTS

- Create a Google ad following the earlier guidance.

- Search for your ad and see where your ad appears in the PageRank (how high a particular page appears following any Google search).

- Remember AdWords is successful because it is based not on how much you paid for the ad, but on how well each ad performs. Ads not relevant to a search will not be clicked on.

How to make your ad relevant and have it clicked on

If you want to sell things online you need to make sure that your advertisement is relevant to the person searching for information about the subject. I am going to discuss how to go about ensuring your ad is at the top of the search results page and explain how to:

- make the right people click on your ad;

- start choosing the best keywords for your site;

- effectively target your ads at the people most likely to become paying customers.

CASE STUDY
Selling a specialist product for a specific group of people – plus size dresses (**www. Annabrooks.com**)

Annabrooks.com is a website that sells dresses to what they call 'plus size' ladies who want to buy formal wear. It is a site for women who need a smart dress for a special occasion – their daughter is getting married, they are going to a black tie dinner or an important work do, for example.

The website owner uses Google AdWords to grow this niche business which she runs at present from home, but plans to expand because 'plus size' is a growing market, particularly in the United States.

The first problem was the name of the site. The URL 'annabrooks.com' is not related to plus size dresses, so she relies on a high 'quality score' from Google to get her website high in the search results. She followed the list of Google's instructions to get a high score when she developed the website:

1   The overall layout and functionality is simple and attractive.

2   It is both easy to navigate and informative.

3   It keeps the user experience in mind.

Here are some ways in which to ensure your website meets those criteria:

- Place important information and images on the top left, where the eye naturally goes first.
- Help people get what they want in three clicks or fewer.
- Cut out pop-ups and pop-unders.
- Create a simple process for users to complete transactions.

Google uses metatags to check that the site has information on it that is relevant to the website's keywords, so the position that she ranks in Google is not just because of how much she paid for the ad but because the site is relevant to the search.

Our first tip is to *make sure your site is built really well* before you begin advertising. When the AdWords sales campaign started, we considered using the most obvious word that would be searched for: 'dresses'. Such a broad keyword would deliver millions of clicks with AdWords, but the dresses sold are all a particular kind of style – conservative, traditional, 'mother of the bride' garments. It was calculated that only a small percentage of the women who type 'dresses' into Google will be plus size women looking for formal wear. So the AdWords that were used instead are much more specific: 'Blue, lacy, mother of the bride, out size dress' gives a top place in the search and when the user clicks on the website it has made a sale in the process.

The owner told me, 'I only want somebody to see my site if they're interested in plus size formal wear. I don't care about anybody else because they are not going to buy anything and that means I'll have paid for a click but I don't get any money back. So even if I had millions of dollars to spend I still wouldn't want to bid on the word "dresses" because the chances are that I would burn through a huge amount of cash and would never make money on that word.'

The owner has another top tip for selling in a niche market. She uses *phrase matching* by putting her keyword phrase between quotations marks – they ensure that the person who sees your ad has searched for the exact words you have written within their search words. She chose phrase matches because she knew they would buy a dress – but of course there is a downside: if she hadn't used quotation marks she would have had a 'broad' match which would have given her more traffic to her site. For plus size dresses a broad match is a high risk strategy and she says it will 'burn through a lot of money' for a small return.

The owner is selling both mother of the bride dresses and holiday party dresses for plus size women, so the website needs different ads targeted for the different sales. With Google, the ad has to be relevant to the keywords, so the owner groups the keywords and writes *ads that are relevant for that group of keywords.* The owner creates three or four different advertisements for a particular group of keywords and then loads them all up into Google and sees which ones generate the most clicks. The popular ads are then served more frequently.

Our final top tip is to *check which ads make you the most money.* This is obvious, but beginners often forget that Google is looking at clicks – that's how it gets its money. It's not looking at sales on your site. You could write an ad that's great in generating clicks but terrible for generating sales – and Google just chooses the one that generates clicks. You need to run the ad that generates sales, such as 'Dress size 30 blue lacy mother of the bride'. We have found that specific phrases create more sales because there aren't that many people searching on AdWords for a size 30 blue lacy mother of the bride dress. The people that do click on this specific ad are very likely to buy the product.

Our last tip is that *specific is cheaper* as you only have to pay Google when someone clicks on your ad. The website does not have to buy many clicks to keep the business healthy and when it does pay Google for clicks, at least the chances are that they will create a sale.

If your advertisement is relevant, Google will charge you less for clicks and your customers will also reward you by buying what you have to sell. If your ads aren't relevant, Google is not the right place for you to advertise. The Google network reaches more than 80 per cent of internet users worldwide. If your ad gets clicked, it is what people are searching for and you have reached the right people. If your ad isn't clicked, it isn't good enough so you will pay more and get a lower place on the page. The best advice in the latter case is to drop the ad altogether – it's a dead duck. The higher your click-through rate – the more people who see your ad and click on it – the less you have to pay for the position you want. This is the basic rule to remember.

Making the right people click on your ad

Imagine that you are selling dresses like Vicki. Say you have bid to pay Google the price of a cup of tea for every person who clicks over to your website. You don't want time-wasters visiting your site because you will still have to pay that cup of tea price for every one of them while not getting any sales. On the other hand, you need to have an attractive advertisement so that genuine potential customers come to your website, not to your competitors who are also selling dresses. To achieve this you have to use the right words in your headline.

A good example of an ad headline – 'Average price plus size dress'. This is a specific headline. It tells you what you are going to get and what the price is.

A bad example – 'Free postage on dresses'. This headline is too attractive. It doesn't 'pre-qualify' your click. People looking for freebies just see the word 'free' and click to see further details. You have paid for them to reach you, but they are a poor prospect because they are looking for something free. They aren't going to buy one of your plus size dresses.

The main elements on the results page are the natural results shown on the main part of the page; but along the right-hand side, and sometimes across the top, is a list of sponsored links. Those sponsored links are the AdWords that the advertisers are buying. So if you type in 'plus size dress', you're going to get 10 sponsored links on the right and occasionally at the top. If there's a very relevant result Google will give it top spot and display it in a different colour.

Google matches the words that someone types into the search to the words that will make your ad appear. These words don't actually have to appear in your ad, but you will have decided which words should trigger the advertisement appearing. For example, your ad might be 'blue dress average price' but some of the words you have chosen to make your ad show for are 'plus size'.

When Mrs Smith searches for 'plus size', the results are displayed on the results page, with 10 sponsored links at the side of the page. If your website plussizedresses is one of these ads and Mrs Smith clicks through to your website, it is at that point that a potential lead has shown an interest and you, the advertiser, will pay a fee for that click depending on what you bid in the auction. You pay Google because each click demonstrates that someone has shown some interest in your ad. When Mrs Smith clicks on your ad it should take her directly to the relevant page of your website, which will tell her more about the product. With any luck she will place an order. Then you make money and everybody is happy.

So, the first thing to do to get your ad to the top of the list of sponsored links is to make sure that your advertisement is relevant.

The importance of relevance and quality in your choice of words

Your first step is to come up with a list of words that people might type in a search that would indicate that they have an interest in buying a plus size dress. Google calls these words 'keywords' and although there are tools within Google to help you choose these, understanding your own business is the most important element of this process. The words you select as keywords are also words that you've probably included already on your website. Things like 'large size', 'extra large', 'plus size', 'mother of the bride' – all the different words that relate to the dresses and buying a special occasion plus size dress. Make a list of all of those keywords and put them into your account.

Google has strict rules about these words and if you break the rules it will disallow your ads. For example, you can't use all capital letters, you can't have more than one exclamation mark, and you can't use somebody else's brand name unless you're actually selling that brand or have some association with that brand. So you can't say, 'Better than Evans outsize clothes' or, 'More choice than Harrods' because you're not associated with those brands. This goes back to Google's motto, 'Don't do evil.' Google wants the page to be as useful as possible to the customers – the people who are doing the search – and when you start using excessive punctuation and lots of 'shouty' capitals it becomes less legible. So you have to be careful not to break their rules.

You usually have only a few seconds to get someone's attention when they are on a page so people have to understand your message very quickly. You can't get very complicated because Google only allows you 25 characters for the headline and 35 for the actual ad, which gives you only a few words, so simplicity and clarity are vital.

Let's take the example of health insurance, which in the United States is quite expensive and is price sensitive. Headlines such as, 'Compare health plan prices, apply online and save' or, 'Get affordable health insurance' are all relevant to the buyers. More important, they also attract people who are ready to buy – someone just looking around as part of a research project, say, would type in 'health insurance' or 'health insurance plans' in their search, but someone actually looking to buy would type in 'affordable insurance' which is more specific. The more accurate the search words, the more likely it is that the person is in buying mode. This is shown in the case study with the words 'mother of the bride plus size dress' and this is the secret of keywords.

Put as many relevant keywords as possible into your account and test them to see which ones work. AdWords has a facility to track your words and over time this enables you to find out which of the words are making you the most money. Then, you can spend more on the most effective keywords and delete those keywords with the least clicks.

You can use negative keywords to make sure that a casual browser or someone looking for a freebie won't see your ad. An example that relates to health insurance would be 'pet' or 'dog' – you only sell human health insurance so you don't want your ad to show when the searcher types 'dog health insurance'.

Before we move on, there are two common mistakes I want to warn you about. The first is omitting important keywords from the advert wording. Not only is this potentially a missed sales opportunity, it also means the campaign loses easy brownie points with Google and may lose its top position. If your business is specific to one area or locality the name of the place will be one of your keywords.

The second is not taking advantage of the local traffic to your site – of course the internet is a global phenomenon, but exciting as it may be to attract visitors from Korea or Australia to your site, it may not be strictly relevant if yours happens to be a man-with-a-van business based in Yorkshire. Fortunately, Google offers you tools to help you localize your web ads, enabling you to target them so that they only attract local traffic. You can use Google's 'geo targeting' for countries, regions and cities, and explain on the website itself any location issues. This is all part of good content design for your website, which in turn comes from knowing which customers you want to attract. Although it's tempting to squash as many keywords as possible into the account, restrict yourself to phrases that really reflect the nature of your business. Go through your website and pick out the most relevant terms. Remember, relevance and accuracy can save you money. The more people who see your ad and click on it, the less you have to pay for the position you want for your ad, because Google rewards popular, relevant ads.

ACTION POINTS

- Ensure your keywords relate to your website. If Google decides that your keywords are not relevant to your website, it won't display it.

- Ads with the keyword in the headline will usually perform better than ones without.

- Have one theme or group of keywords called an 'ad group' for each ad.

- When writing your ads, make sure you don't flout Google's rules, so do not use multiple exclamation marks or UNNECESSARY capital letters!

- The more accurate the search words typed into Google, the more likely a person is to be in buying mode. Put yourself in the frame of mind of your potential customers and try to specifically match their possible searches.

> Use the AdWords facility that allows you to track which of your keywords have been most successful and which have resulted in actual sales. Delete the least successful ads.

> You can use an AdWords setting that means your ad will only be seen if someone searches for the exact words you have written. But beware: although this means that you maximize the chances of click-throughs resulting in sales, you also runs the risk of missing out on genuine potential customers who type in a slightly different search.

Different methods of selling online

There are as many ways to make money online as there are creative people coming up with new ideas. It's not only about selling *things*; you can just as easily make money online by selling ideas.

CASE STUDY
Selling a seasonal product –
goose for Xmas lunch (**http://www.empirefarm.co.uk/**)

Empire Farm is a 100-acre organic farm on the edge of the Blackmore Vale, just south of Wincanton in Somerset. For the past five years the farmers Sally and Adrian Morgan have been raising organic geese, ducks, chickens, turkeys, sheep and pigs – mostly traditional but some rare breeds. The products available vary during the year, and meat from the animals can be purchased from the online shop. Sally Morgan has used Google AdWords to sell organic geese in the run-up to Christmas.

Sally and Adrian are what they call 'new farmers'. Sally is a teacher and runs courses on how to be a smallholders or poultry keeper. She spends her life managing the farm office, looking after the animals and running the courses; and then at Christmas she sells organic geese for the Christmas market. The geese are plucked and dressed on the farm and then sent by mail to the customer.

The business started from nothing and at Sally's second Christmas on the farm she had 150 geese to sell and no experience of direct marketing. She began by advertising online and quickly found the keywords that worked – 'We found them so successful I've had little need to change them too much.' But she also keeps a close eye on her competitors. She recognizes that, 'There is not a huge amount of competition in the marketplace for us. So getting our position on the page is not too difficult for us, particularly as we mention the word "organic".'

She spends a little more than the price of a pair of shoes a week on words such as 'Empire Farm goose', 'Luxury organic goose for Christmas,' and 'organic limited supplies'. So far the words 'luxury organic goose for Christmas, limited numbers' has achieved the most hits, but Wincanton is not an affluent area of Somerset; organic goose selling at about a third of a price of a pair of shoes per kilo was a higher price than the local market would pay. Sally said, 'They would just laugh and say they would get a whole goose for much less. So we knew we had to look for more affluent markets beyond our home area. We looked at alternative ways of online marketing and suddenly realized that AdWords was a very good way of working.'

Sally thinks that she has been successful because at Christmas customers are prepared to search online to get something special. Her business is niche – there are only 10 or 12 people selling goose at Christmas online so she is not competing against hundreds of other pages showing organic geese for sale.

After the first couple of years selling online she noticed that there was a reluctance among customers to pick up the phone and follow the order through. 'I don't know whether I'm right but I feel that the person who has done their searching online, has got their credit card in their hand and just want to get the job done. They don't want to have to ring and order through the phone.' So Sally created a shopping facility on the website. She bought a ready-made package for online shopping – 'It was dead easy to do,' she says. 'The "World Pay" at the end is taken care of by an agency, through the bank and it is very easy to maintain.'

She has some top tips for other entrepreneurs who plan to sell in a niche market online. The first is to pay attention to the information on the website as well as selling. She thinks that people like to read about the products and she puts special effort into making sure the Empire Farm website reflects her values – friendly, approachable and organic. She aims for the site to be more than just a shop front; it's a place where the customer can see what's happening on the farm and what a good life the animals have had. This makes good business sense because the customer will pay more for organic geese – and they can see videos online of the geese running around in the field. Her view is that with remote purchase the customers need to trust the website that they are buying from, and she wants to clearly show the welfare standards on the farm.

Sally's second tip is to research competitors and see what words they are using. She says, 'I'm quite nosy. I will look when I'm in the browser to see which keywords they are using in their metatags.'

Sally is working hard to re-establish orchards at her farm so she can graze geese under the apple trees in the traditional manner. And she may even attempt some cider making.... Sounds like a good combination with the geese!

Before you do anything else and before you start spending money on your ads, it's important to stop and consider exactly what kind of business you are running. From there you can start to understand who your customers might be and what they might type into a Google search. There are broadly four different kinds of online business, discussed below.

1. Physical product

This is the most simple and straightforward online business. Sally Morgan had the product (150 geese ready for Christmas dinner); she just needed customers. Now she is selling educational courses to customers who would like to keep their own poultry, so she has moved into a service industry. Amazon was one of the early pioneers of e-commerce and it originally concentrated on selling books online. But as the internet evolved, Amazon moved with the times and now you can buy anything on its site, from books to music, cookery equipment, clothes, jewellery and even sex aids!

People are now much more comfortable about purchasing items online and, perhaps surprisingly, items such as shoes and clothes have become big business. Companies such as zappos.com (a US online shoe company) work hard to provide the very best customer service to encourage people to buy online. Naturally, if you are buying any kind of clothing from the internet you cannot be totally sure that it will fit, so companies such as these make sure that they offer very simple returns policies to give total peace of mind to their customers.

2. Non-physical product

As the name suggests, these are products that do not have any physical components and would include things like car insurance, home insurance and health insurance. A customer can search online, research all the different aspects and costs of policies for a range of companies, and then complete the transaction online.

3. Lead generation

This is a relatively new class of online product and it quite often deals with what are termed 'big needs' – buying a house or a car, for example. Obviously, these are huge, important purchases that people will not want to make without first seeing the actual product, so lead generation is a kind of 'product' that provides information that can eventually drive people to physically visit car dealerships to see a car or to estate agents to view a house. Such websites are not *selling* products; they are providing information that *could lead to* the sale of a product. Car dealers in particular are willing to spend a lot of money providing information online that will convince people to come and visit their dealership to purchase a car.

4. Physical service

If you run a small business that is, for example, involved in watch repair, you are offering a service that cannot be completed online. But you might want to advertise your service online so that local people will visit your premises. This works in a similar way to how people would use *Yellow Pages*. Someone has a broken watch; they search online and find your ad with details about your local service. You can specifically target your local area and provide contact information that will result in enquiries to your business, whether it's a watch repair shop, a hairdressers or a dry cleaning service.

'Hard disk recovery services' represent one of the most expensive clicks on AdWords for this kind of business. People will search these kinds of keywords if their computer has crashed and they are absolutely desperate to get it fixed and retrieve their valuable data. The cost for these clicks is high – as much as two cups of coffee in the United States – simply because anyone clicking on that link is almost definitely going to become a paying customer.

Using your product as a test case

If you are setting up a new company or perhaps seeking to expand your existing company, you might want to discover how big your potential market is before committing too much money, especially if your idea needs significant investment to get it into motion.

Understandably, you'd like a reasonable idea of your chances of success.

Let's use a shoe repair shop as an example. A quick and cost-effective way of taking the pulse of the sort of demand there might be for such a shop in your area is to set up a simple, one-page website that contains the basic details about your company. Then set up an AdWords account to advertise it. The volume of clicks over perhaps a three- or four-week period would tell you a lot about the viability of the business. If only one person visited your site you may decide it's not a good investment. But if a few dozen or more reached your landing page, then you're in business! Easy. A quick and simple way of testing the water without having to part with a lot of cash. Try it!

Enticing your customers

Let's say that you have done your bit of AdWords market research. You have decided that your new shoe repair business is a good prospect and you name your new venture, 'Fancy Footwork'. The immediate problem here is that your new 'brand' is not known by anybody. There is no chance that anyone is going to type 'Fancy Footwork Shoe Repair' into a Google search, unless your Mum wants to see your website. So, instead of using the name of your business in your ads, you need to focus on the problem you are solving – fixing broken shoes – rather than the name of your service.

Let's use another example and say that you are a life coach and you want to expand your clientele – after all, you are so successful that many of your clients have now left because you have helped them to lead happy, fulfilling lives! There are two ways in which Google can help you. First, 'Google search': if someone actively searches for career development or personal development, your ad will appear on the results page if you have chosen your keywords carefully. Second, 'Google content network': your potential customers may not be actively searching for the service you offer, but you are placing a link to your services right in front of the very people most interested in what you are selling.

The beautiful thing about AdWords is that you only have to pay if someone actually clicks on your link. You only pay for people who are interested in whatever it is you are selling. Being displayed on a search results page or, as in our life coaching example, on a site that discusses life coaching, doesn't actually cost you a penny until someone clicks that link to your website. Brilliant, isn't it?

ACTION POINTS

- Establish what kind of business you are running. Is it a product or a service?

- Determine the need you are aiming to meet for your customers.

- If you are unsure about your market, set up a simple web page and basic AdWords campaign to test the water.

- If you are offering a brand new product or service, focus your ads on the need you are meeting or the problem you are solving, not the name of your company that nobody has yet heard of.

- To help reach those potential paying customers, use AdWords' tools to target your ads to specific geographical areas or even particular times of the day.

- Try to include a call to action in your ads to really give people a shove towards your website. Make it active, not passive.

CHAPTER 3

Sophisticated online tricks of the trade

In this chapter you are going to learn the sophisticated online tricks of the trade to make your business even more successful online. I am going to show you case studies that explain how to set up your business for an international market. You'll be learning the easy methods to:

- research competitors and customers online;
- generate leads and entice customers for big ticket items;
- maintain the quality of your advertisement;
- sell intangibles;
- use Google Analytics to find out the facts and figures that will help you grow your business.

How to research competitors online

Google AdWords is a tremendous tool for researching a potential market for a new business. So it makes sense to set up a small one- or two-page website, beginning an AdWords campaign and then working out if you business is going to be a success.

It is something that you can set up remarkably quickly and run for a few days. For example, imagine you are setting up a flower shop in a small town. Your website could be a single page with some useful information about the imminent debut of the new venture, such as:

- the name of the business;
- some basic contact details;
- information on the kind of occasions your flower arrangements can cover;
- how quickly flowers can be delivered;
- details of a special opening week promotion.

You can run the ads and the website for a few days, using your special keywords and asking Google to only show your ads to people searching in your geographical area. Quite quickly, you could start to develop an idea of the volume of clicks your business might receive. You are not completely misleading the people searching because, hopefully, in the future they might return to take advantage of your service. If the ads are not delivering a lot of volume then you might want to reconsider the business, but if you are receiving a lot of hits then you may have struck gold!

Naturally, this won't produce data as accurate as the real business will deliver, but it will give you a decent idea of the kind of market out there and how effective your idea might be.

Paying for your ads

When you begin your first AdWords campaign, Google will suggest a fairly high price to start with. This will help to ensure you have a decent spot on the search results page and you can start receiving the volume of clicks your business needs to get going. Remember, though, to set a daily spending limit on your campaign.

Even if you are testing a few basic keywords to see how they might perform, you need to stop thinking of a budget in terms of a cup of coffee or a pair of shoes, but the cost of a new suit. Much less than that and you will not really be testing your idea stringently enough or giving it enough chance to succeed.

However, if your ads are receiving plenty of clicks thanks to your attractive copy and your smart targeting and if the relevance to the page you are directing people to is high, then Google will begin to rate your ad highly because it is delivering what Google users need. Once that happens, you will start to receive a discount on your ads.

Let's return to our new flower business. Your ad might read something like:

Beautiful Flowers

Fast, reliable delivery

All occasions, order now!

Flos-Flowers.com

The keywords that you might be targeting would be something like: 'quick flower delivery' or 'immediate flowers'. This is a competitive business, so it might cost you perhaps the price of a cup of coffee per click. At this stage, Google does not know how relevant or how good your ad might be, but after a few days of receiving dozens or even hundreds of clicks (so you have to be prepared to make an investment here) Google will begin to calculate that your ad is rather effective.

This is great news because if Google is impressed with the quality of your ad it will give it a boost in the rankings *without any increase in the price you are paying*. It's the beauty of AdWords – you are rewarded for your smart wording and attention to relevancy as well as the money you are willing to invest. If your original ad was sixth on the list of the search results page, you might see it boosted to second or third if it is performing well and, obviously, the higher your ad in the rankings, the more clicks you'll receive and the more business you'll get. Then you can start to make a calculation yourself. If the amount of business you were receiving while your ad was placed sixth was pretty high, you might decide to reduce your bid for each click and keep your ad in that position because you don't feel you need to be top of the rankings to make your business work.

Managing your data

A common mistake when it comes to altering your campaigns, whether it's the wording of your ads, the choice of keywords or the amount you are paying for clicks, is to make decisions before enough data are available.

If your ad is receiving one or two clicks per day, it is dangerous to start making changes because you cannot be sure that those clicks are representative of your potential clientele. A good rule of thumb is to wait until you have at least a hundred clicks on an ad before making any changes, otherwise you are guessing what is working rather than relying on hard data.

Yet again, Google is here to help, particularly when you are starting out. It is easy to be unsure about the wording of your ad in these early times and you'll have understandable doubts, so a good strategy is to write 10 different ads and feed them into the AdWords system. Within these ads you can try different words, different phrases and different combinations and experiment with that all-important call-to-action. Google will then rotate those ads for you on the results pages. Over a period of time it will work out which ones are performing best and will start to use those ads above the ones that have been less successful.

It's a service that doesn't cost you any extra money because, as always, you only pay for actual clicks to your website. Your AdWords account is made up of your campaigns and each campaign has a daily spending limit. Within those campaigns you have your ad groups and each group has a set of keywords and a set of ads to run against them. A maximum of 50 ads per group is a decent number to test with, and once you have some results you can begin to delete the ones that have performed poorly.

The problem is that it can take a lot of time to collect enough data on an individual keyword to decide whether you should persist with it or how much you should be bidding for it. The solution is to bid for a group of keywords so that you can reach a larger chunk of data faster than you would for an individual keyword.

Let's use our flower shop to illustrate the point. Within one ad group you decide to use the keywords: 'fast flower delivery', 'immediate flower delivery' and 'quick flower delivery'. These are all similar keywords. For the first you might receive 40 clicks, for the second you might receive 20 clicks and for the third you might get another 40 clicks. Individually, there's not really enough there to make an informed decision on how well they're working, but if you add them together in the same ad group you have 100 clicks, which means you can set an accurate bid for the ad group as a whole and it will apply to all your keywords in the group. In effect, you're pooling your data to allow you to make a smarter decision on the investment you're making in your ads.

Then you can start to burrow even deeper. Try to keep keywords that perform similarly in one ad group. For instance, if 'immediate flower delivery' is netting you a high rate of conversions to actual sales, but 'fast flower delivery' is receiving a lower conversion rate, take 'fast flower delivery' out of that ad group and build another group based around the word 'fast' that you can bid a little less for. These seemingly small changes can really save you money!

Once you have set up your ads and you are beginning to see positive results, you may not need to manage them quite so strictly. If the ads are producing sales, it might just need the odd little tweak here and there to keep the ship steady, but largely Google will handle all the heavy lifting and you can sit back with a cup of tea and give yourself a pat on the back for an ad well written.

Even then, it pays to keep an eye out for particular fads and trends that might end up driving extra business your way. A sudden heatwave might see a sharp rise in sales of sandals, for example, so an online shoe shop might quickly run a new ad:

Cool your feet!

Summer sandals are here

Next day delivery, order now

SheilaShoes.com

Other events, of course, you will be able to see coming. With our flower shop all it would need is a brief check of the calendar. Mother's Day is always a date that flower shops thrive on, so perhaps even in January you might decide to start running ads for Mother's Day flower deliveries. Then you can start being really clever because the link on your ad could take a customer to a page with a series of special Mother's Day offers, which will please Google for its relevancy and therefore keep your ad nice and high in the rankings.

Gathering data about your customers and competitors

As your business continues to gather pace you can begin to think about using your website to capture additional data about the people who visit. One way is to encourage visitors to leave their e-mail address or phone number so that they can be contacted about special offers or deals.

Another is to use a sound clip or video clip that people can listen to or view to learn more about your product or service. You can monitor how well such an application is performing by the number of downloads it receives. It's all part of developing your website and becoming truly focused on exactly fulfilling your customers' needs.

The whole process around AdWords relies on your being flexible and imaginative and willing to try all the different tricks that I've explained throughout this book. So what are you waiting for? Get out there and start!

ACTION POINTS

- Be prepared to invest a few hundred pounds in your AdWords campaign to start with to give your ads a chance of succeeding. An ad that is popular and relevant will end up saving you money, because Google will give it a boost in the rankings due to its effectiveness.

- Wait until you receive at least 100 clicks on an ad before chopping and changing your wording. Receiving one sale from one click does not tell you anything: the next 99 clicks may yield no sales at all.

- You can ask AdWords to rotate a new set of ads and work out for itself which are the most effective.

- Group sets of similar keywords together in one ad group so that you can accumulate useful data about their performance more quickly and make an informed decision about the amount you should be paying for a click.

- Keep your eyes peeled for topical fads or relevant dates in the calendar – you might want to produce limited-time ads to cash in on them.

Lead generation and enticing customers for big ticket items

You want to reach your customers at the precise moment that they want to buy the product or service you are offering. You need to know what your competitors are doing in the marketplace so that you can maximize your ability to:

- tell your audience what your product or service is;

- highlight its benefits;

- choose the right words, the right phrases, and the right *number* of words and phrases that will bring customers to your site;

- expand your list of keywords;

- use online tools to help you generate variations on your keywords.

CASE STUDY
Using a website to generate leads for cosmetic and plastic surgeons in California

Helene Gryfakis is a Price per Click Marketing Director based in the United States and managed the AdWords account for a cosmetic and plastic surgery group in Beverly Hills, California. The company has a wide range of services including breast implants, tummy tucks, liposuction, rhinoplasty, facelifts and other plastic surgery procedures. The business uses certified plastic surgeons and also provides gastric banding for clients with weight issues and podiatry doctors for painful foot problems.

Helene's aim was to utilize the group's website for generating leads for the business. She discovered that key AdWords for cosmetic surgery are both expensive and competitive. The cosmetic surgery group was using AdWords at a high cost with not much return. Words such as 'liposuction', 'breast implant' or 'breast augmentation' were expensive and Helene stated that many people were clicking on the ads but no one was buying, and the fixed sum set for marketing was running out by lunchtime each day. She said, 'The business was running through the set budget quickly in the morning and then there would be no ads running the rest of the day. The site was ranking high for non-converting keywords.'

So Helene's first task was to sort through the ranking keywords and discover which ads were successful. The strategy worked well and within a month of taking over the campaign the average cost per lead dropped by almost two-thirds. Equally important, the number of potential customers doubled.

Helene's key piece of advice is to develop multiple ads. She proved to the cosmetic surgery company that it is not enough to write one ad for a group of words. With one advertisement you can't compare which ad is working best and discover which ads are more compelling. She wrote six ads for an ad group and made each one slightly different. She suggested that there should be slightly different offers, a slightly different call to action, and different wording; then she could assess which ads had a higher click-through and conversion. Every week she would compile a list of the top performing ads and pause the low performing ones.

What made the entire project unusual was that some of the cosmetic surgeons had appeared on popular US TV shows about plastic surgery, including 'Dr 90210', 'Access Hollywood', 'Entertainment Tonight' and the 'Tyra Banks Show'. Helene realized that 'as seen on TV' or 'Dr 90210' was a less expensive AdWord than 'breast enhancement', so she began to test new AdWords based on subjects the TV programmes were featuring. On one programme insurance issues were discussed, and she would promote insurance as an element of the ads. Many plastic surgeons do not take patients using insurance, so identifying insurance as a call to action became a compelling element of the advertisement. Alternatively, she would focus on location, and the geographical situation of the clinic in Beverly Hills became an important part of the advertisement. Another successful keyword was 'top surgeon'. As soon as one of the surgeons featured on a TV show, many of the viewers decided that he was the man to fix their problem – so they would search against the programme titles and they would click to the ad featuring his name. She said, 'We'd focus on the actual surgeons because their names were high profile. Then we were able to see which ads converted the best just from all the different call to actions though our testing.'

After two years, the Google Ads were fine-tuned and the cost per conversion dropped again. Helene's view is that analysing the data and making changes daily will make a significant difference to the cost per click. 'The only way you will get ahead with Google AdWords is by looking at the data every day. If you just let it run on the default, your ad is displayed but not targeted. You may get people just clicking but they don't have a serious interest. So you're paying for nothing. Checking your keywords in order to make sure the keyword is converting will make sure that your ad spend is cost effective.'

Cosmetic surgery is a big business and the group discovered that their competitors copied their strategy. Helene found that as soon as she had a successful ad, a competitor would copy her campaign and keywords. Her advice is to avoid bidding for the number one position unless it is part of a particular plan, such as a short-term promotion, in order to save money that would be spent out-bidding the competition. In her experience the customers click the first advertisement and the second advertisement, but it is the third advertisement that converts to a sale. Her analysis showed that between second and fourth place provided serious customers for the cosmetic surgery group. And she certainly has a happy face!

Reaching customers who are ready to buy

Every customer goes through a series of stages in his or her mind before taking the plunge and paying for a product or service. It's what we might call the 'purchasing cycle'. Obviously, the bigger the purchase, the more thought will go into it, but there are identifiable stages that are common to any purchase.

The cycle starts when someone begins to think about a product they might need. At this stage, your ad may be of some interest to them, but they are not ready to part with their cash.

Next follows a stage of research, where the potential customer will look into the product and compare costs and features and, increasingly these days, will consult opinions online from customers who have bought similar products. Again, your ad will be of interest to them, but a click-through may still not result in a sale.

Finally, your potential customer reaches that golden 'purchasing stage', when they have their credit or debit card glinting in their hand and they are ready to do business. This is the optimum moment when you want them to see your ad and click-through to your website. These are the people you are looking to attract and you need to make sure you are paying the right amount for that visitor.

When a person reaches this stage, they are likely to be typing in 'trigger' words, such as 'buy', 'purchase' or 'need'. These kinds of words signal that the searcher is ready to become a paying customer, so when these words are typed alongside your kind of product, you need your ad to appear as high up the Google search results page as possible. Depending on how fierce your competition is, these words can become expensive but in the long run it is a good investment because clicks that result from these searches are far more likely to earn you a sale.

If the searcher uses words such as 'compare' or 'price', they are still in the research stage. That still means that you want your ad to appear to these people because you want to be included in their research, but at the same time you don't want to be paying as much as you would for the key trigger words that indicate a more imminent purchase.

Once your ad appears following a search you need to try every little trick to encourage people to select your ad above any other ad on the list. If your ad appears but people don't tend to click on it, Google notes this, decides that it's not relevant enough and it begins to drop down the list.

One way to grab the attention of your potential customer is to use a Google AdWords tool that allows you to replace the headline of your ad with the precise words of the relevant search. This is effective because it immediately shows the searcher that you have *exactly* what they want.

Let's just have a look at how this works. Imagine you wanted to sell pizza and your ad was typed like this:

Ad text

{Keyword: Great Pizza}

Delicious Secret Sauce

Pepperoni Petes. Fill your tum!

PetesPizza.com

Then, if someone searched for 'Norwich Pizza Delivery', the ad would appear on the results page like this:

Norwich Pizza Delivery

Delicious Secret Sauce

Pepperoni Petes. Fill your tum!

PetesPizza.com

It's the same ad, but it has been individually tailored to the person who typed the search, making it more attractive. If the search term is greater than the 25 characters allowed, then the ad simply reverts to your original 'Great Pizza' headline.

Use your words carefully – be succinct and clear and remember that all-important 'call to action', which has a really significant effect on how a potential customer reacts to an ad. Don't be shy in highlighting the benefits of your product in your ad. If your pizza is the cheapest in the area, say so. If you use a special tomato sauce passed down from your Italian ancestors, let people know ... but just find a way of saying it in five or six words! Use punchy, interesting phrases that will make your ad stand out from the crowd.

Expanding your list of keywords

Once you've written your first ad and you've chosen a couple of key-words, the next stage is to expand your list and start to find ways of reaching more and more potential customers.

Let's say that one of the keywords you have chosen for your pizza business is simply, 'pizza'. This is a common internet search word because pizza is a popular food item that people are willing to order online. But if someone simply types in that single word as a search, they could be typing it for any number of reasons. They might want to know how to make pizza, the average calorie count of a Hawaiian pizza, where they can buy frozen pizza or they may even be researching the origins of this wonderful Italian food! Are you feeling as hungry as I am?

The point is that people who type such a broad search may not be interested in buying a pizza at all. That's not to say you shouldn't run an ad with that keyword, but because you cannot possibly be sure what the searcher is after it's not worth paying a lot of money for it.

The point of your ad is to attract as many profitable clicks as possible, so your aim has to be to gather all the words you can think of that someone who wants to buy a pizza might type into Google. One way might be to use the word 'pizza' in combination with all the different toppings that you offer: 'pizza pepperoni', 'pizza mushrooms', 'pizza vegetarian', 'pizza meat lovers' and so on. You are trying to match more specific searches – searches that are likely to result in sales.

Next you could consider the different styles of pizza on offer: 'deep dish pizza', 'filled-crust pizza', or 'authentic stone-baked pizza'. And if you're really smart you may be able to find a little niche area that no one has thought of that doesn't contain your main keyword, whether that's pizza, watch repair or life coaching. Perhaps you might include a keyword for 'garlic bread' or, for those real Italian aficionados you want to target, how about 'calzone'? The advantage of finding niche words that other companies might not think of using is that you won't need to pay so much to get your ad at the top of the results page.

Slowly, you can expand your keywords in this way and eventually graduate to using three- or four-word keyword combinations that can be very profitable. Let's just break this down a bit so you can see what I mean:

> **Keyword: Pizza** – This is very general and unlikely to result in a sale.

Keyword: Pepperoni pizza – This is better. It's more specific and shows that the searcher has a little more idea about what they're after.

Keyword: Buy pepperoni pizza – Now we're getting somewhere. What you have here is someone *willing to buy a pizza*. You can comfortably pay more for this search because the likelihood of a sale is higher.

Keyword: Buy Pepperoni Pizza in Norwich – This is perfect (as long as your business is in Norwich!) You have a hungry customer in your area who wants pizza. Naturally, this is a search that will not appear as often as simply 'pizza', but your click-through rates and conversion to sales rates are going to be much higher. Your service is exactly relevant to the search, so you can bid more money and stand a much better chance of appearing at the top of Google's results page. Remember, it is safe to bid higher because you don't pay Google anything unless someone clicks on your link.

As your list expands, you'll be able to tell which ads are netting you the most profits and which are not performing quite so well and adjust the prices you are paying for clicks accordingly. It's just as important to pay the right price for your clicks as it is to get your clicks in the first place.

Helpful tools

Thinking up all these keywords may sound a little tough. It's not. You don't need to sit there for hours racking your brain for all the different variations that fit your product, because happily Google is here to help. Simply click the 'Keyword Tool' button in your AdWords account and type in your first keyword – for example, 'pizza'. This helpful tool will immediately report back to you with all kinds of synonyms and variations that people may type into a search engine when looking to buy a pizza.

Private companies can offer a similar kind of service along with further analysis and useful statistics that will help you choose the perfect words for your ad. Usually these services offer a free limited-time trial so you can decide for yourself how handy their service might be for your needs. One example is Word Tracker, which helps you to understand the kind of volume of searches particular words receive. For instance, you might discover that the word 'pizza' is receiving 37 million global searches, with around two-thirds of them in the United States, while 'Italian pizza' is getting just 90,000 searches. Once more, it's clear that being specific pays dividends. 'Pizza' gets millions of searches and your small business may be lost in the shuffle, but 'Italian pizza' is more of a niche that your business may be able to take advantage of.

Another site worth visiting is Keyword Discovery, which can help you research words that perform successfully and can suggest alternative terms or phrases you may not have considered.

So you can see that there are two quite distinct skills to creating something approaching the perfect ad. The first is the creative part, where you attempt to write a clever, punchy ad that will outshine your competitors, and the second is the analytical side of locating the right keywords, honing them, and discovering the exact amount of cash you should pay for each individual click. Once you've finished reading this book, you'll be an expert in both!

Maintaining the quality of your ad

Google offers a lot of clever little tricks that allow you to narrow down your audience and target, as far as possible, those most likely to buy your product. When a search is made Google can roughly locate the area where the computer is located, so you can instruct AdWords to only show your ad to those people in your immediate area, or you can limit the times of day when you want your ad to appear.

However, there are more factors that count towards your ad's positioning on the results page than how much you pay and the relevance of your keywords. Google's system is intuitive, smart and powerful and is able to study the correlation between the wording on your ad and the wording on the web page that your ad links to.

For example, let's say that your pizza ad is as follows:

Great Pizza

Best quality pepperoni

Quick service, buy now!

PetesPizza.com

Now, if the web page that this ad sends the customer to is actually a page about pasta then there is a 'disconnect' between what the ad is claiming and what the page is actually about. Even if your site sells great quality pepperoni pizza, if the page you are sending people to does not mention it, Google will lower your quality score and it can cost you a high spot on the results page. However, if your link takes customers to a page that explains just why your pepperoni is the best and lists your variety of pepperoni pizzas and how much they are, Google will give you a higher quality score for your landing page and your ad will remain prominent on the results page.

Think carefully about the ads you are buying. If you run a very small website, ensure that all your ads are relevant to the information on your site. If you have a larger website, you can be very specific about which pages you direct people to. For example, if a person is searching for vegetarian pizza, make sure your ad for veggie pizzas has a link that directs them to your specialist veggie-pizza-only page.

Keep everything tight and relevant and Google will reward your honesty. Remember: Google is interested in serving its customers the best way it can. It is not interested in advertisers who fool people into visiting sites that don't contain the kind of information they're looking for.

Google wants people to get what they want as simply as possible. And that's what you want too! So be as helpful as you can in guiding people to the right parts of your site.

ACTION POINTS

- Try to find words that your competitors may not think of using to establish your own advertising niche. This can be surprisingly effective and is also likely to be cheaper than relying on common, established words.

- Customers who type in 'trigger' words such as 'buy' or 'purchase' into a search engine are most likely to become paying customers, so make sure you bid high for those clicks.

- Expand your keywords to include all the different words, phrases and permutations someone might type into Google if they are interested in buying your product or service.

- Matching specific keywords to specific searches maximizes the chances of attracting a customer ready to make a purchase.

- Utilize online tools such as AdWords' Keyword Tool or Word Tracker to help you think of new keywords and study the effectiveness of different words and phrases.

- Always ensure that your ad and the web page your ad links to are relevant to each other. Google will then keep your quality score nice and high.

Selling in a virtual world – how to sell things that don't exist!

The internet is an exciting place, full of opportunities for creative people. As well as physical products, you can sell virtual ones, and get paid in virtual money – which can be turned into hard cash in the real world.

One of the great successes of recent years is the rise of internet gaming, and in particular social networking games sites like Second Life and IMVU, where people take on different characters or 'avatars', and enjoy a separate existence in a virtual world. You can be whoever you want to be, live in the kind of home you've always dreamt of, change your looks at will, meet and interact with other people, and – most interesting for the budding online entrepreneur – *shop* online to furnish your apartment or dress in style.

It's a bit like dressing-up games for adults – though there are now also virtual life sites catering for younger teenagers and children too. These sites are for people to have fun and indulge their fantasies, but there are also money-making opportunities here. Although transactions take place in the virtual world, the most successful games players are making real money out of designing virtual products – some of them reportedly earning as much as fashion designers in the real world.

Want to have a go? It's a fun way of selling online and who knows, you could strike lucky and become a Valentino of a virtual world. Through the following case study you'll learn:

- the sites to look out for;
- how to make pocket money from your creations that you can spend on site;
- the way to create a look that earns you significant wealth in the real world too.

CASE STUDY

Spike Sieghardt, games player, makes money through creativity (**www.imvu.com**)

Spike Sieghardt doesn't give away much about himself – his real self, that is. He allowed us to know that he was born in Minnesota in the United States, and lives in the Twin Cities. Everything else about him – age, past career, hair colour – is a blank, and he likes to keep it that way, though he did let slip that he had done a college course in graphic design, and worked with CAD software.

'The thing that always appealed to me about the internet is that you can be whoever you want to be,' says Spike. 'I've been involved in the online gaming community for years. But it wasn't until I came across Second Life that I really felt at home – my second home, of course! I could create an entire new being for myself – one of many, if I felt like it. I could be a poet, a rock star, a high-rolling banker, an assassin, even a woman if the fancy took me.'

Spike was fascinated by the different looks he could create for himself. As well as Second Life, he registered as a social networking player on a site called IMVU. 'It's one of the easiest to use if you're a creator,' he says. 'When you first enter the site, you choose a name for yourself, and a basic avatar, and they give you a thousand free credits to shop for clothes to individualize your look. But that's only the beginning. As soon as you start playing seriously you personalize everything – body type, hair style and colour, the clothes you wear, your online home, your wheels. You sign up for an online account and credits to spend in virtual shops. After a while you get to know the designers that create the looks you like, and you go back to their carts over and over. You wouldn't believe it from my avatar, but in real life I'm kind of a dull dresser – jeans, T-shirt, loafers – but online I like to let rip. At first I was into that 80's Kiss look – monochrome make-up and jump suits. When I couldn't find stuff exactly the way I wanted it, I began designing my own online outfits, and the people I was interacting with on the site started asking where they could buy similar styles. So I started selling to them.'

At first Spike just made a few credits here and there, which he spent on the site. But as he grew more confident, he broadened his range of designs. 'I got heavily into more Goth looks,' he says. 'Somehow that struck a chord, and word spread. I was selling a lot to online vampires. Before long I was picking up more credits than I could spend online, and I started converting them to real money.' He's cagey about what he actually earns from selling online designs. 'It's nowhere near as much as the big guys, who make hundreds of thousands of dollars a year. But put it this way, it's more than I earn from my day job.'

So how do you follow Spike's example? 'It's a growing field,' says Mark Harnett, former marketing director of IMVU. 'There are quite a few social networking games sites now, and on ones like ours and Second Life people are spending and making money. Part of the fun of the game is selecting your avatar's look, and we have over 4 million items in our catalogue. Anything you can imagine, it's there to buy online – clothes, hairstyles, eye colours, skin colour, make-up, jewellery, tattoos, furniture, rooms....'

Any means of expressing yourself in a virtual world is available. The reason IMVU's catalogue is so big is that almost all of the items in it are created by individual site users, who sell their virtual designs to other site users. They sell under their avatar names, so if a buyer sees something they like in the catalogue, they know who has created it and they can search in future for that creator's cart. Each seller earns credits, which they can use online or sell on to convert to real money. In other words, IMVU has created a whole virtual economy.

It helps if you have a graphics or computer-aided design background, but it's by no means necessary. 'There are more than a hundred thousand creators on IMVU who are creating things,' says Mark. 'Most people do it at a hobbyist level because it's fun to create new room colours or T-shirt designs – that's pretty straightforward. A handful at the top are making a lot of money – many of them 3D graphic arts people who are able to create unbelievably realistic images.'

As with so many other online enterprises, the key is to work with what you love. If you care about your product and put enthusiasm and energy into it, other people will care too and buy it. Cynics need not apply.

But how do you make the leap from small-time site user selling to friends, to top-flight designer making serious money? The trick is to follow Spike's example and find a niche market that helps you establish a reputation among enthusiasts. You should search for a corner of the market that will be yours – a look and style that you like yourself, and that will allow you to express your creativity.

'You have to go and play on the world first and find your niche,' says Mark. 'Then you can go on to create products that satisfy the demand for that niche. It might be bikers and leather and tattoos, or it might be disco neon. There are many different niche communities on sites like IMVU, and they are willing to buy a lot of stuff if you can create looks that appeal to them.'

Don't be afraid of starting small. You shouldn't spread yourself too thinly by struggling to create a huge and varied portfolio of designs. You will do much better to start off with a few unusual items that will appeal to like-minded people. Once you have established a reputation, then you can really let your imagination loose. The virtual world is your oyster!

ACTION POINTS

- Play on the site until you understand how it works.
- Start small and simple.
- Sell to your friends first – let them help you create a reputation.
- Find your niche.
- Sell what you love.
- Build on your successes – don't be content with pocket money, but see if you can attract a wider following for your ideas.

Analytics

Although the online world is very creative, you should not ignore the business opportunities that can be developed around numbers and analysis. If you click into the standard Google AdWords Campaign Manager you will have found a good reporting system that tells you about clicks and impressions and how well your different ads are doing; but it doesn't tell you a lot about how your actual website is performing. If you want further information you can turn to Google Analytics. This is a very simple to use web analytics tool that is free. Sign up for it inside your AdWords account in the reporting area and add some very simple pieces of HTML to your website.

CASE STUDY
Analysing how to sell shoes (**www.schuh.co.uk**)

Schuh is a shoe retailer with 50 stores on the UK high street and a big website that sells footwear online. Schuhstore.co.uk has around 400,000 different people visiting each month and has increased the number of people buying shoes on its site by using a few simple techniques. Schuh uses Google information to discover where the customers have been on the site and is continually upgrading and changing the site so that customers can use it more easily. It believes that sales and marketing and IT and finance are all part of the same function – improving the customers experience so they buy more shoes!

Schuh's basic approach is to continually test its website and change it to make sure that it works for the customers. People buy more than one pair of shoes in a lifetime so it plans to have more than just one sale – ideally it would like what it calls 'lifetime' value from each customer, and for that it needed answers to some simple questions:

- Does the website work?
- Does the link get you to where you want to be?
- Does it give you the shoes you want to buy?

Because Schuh has real-life stores as well as a website it has taken expertise from its shops to the online experience. Shoes don't sell in a cluttered space, so it doesn't clutter the site. Just as the till is easy to find in the shop, so the checkout is easy to find on the website. It doesn't make customers fill in forms before they are allowed to buy shoes in the shop, so it doesn't bother them online. The online experience is closely connected to the actual stores – so you can buy online and take the item back to any Schuh store, check stock availability in any of the 50 stores online, and transfer stock from branch to branch.

Schuh thinks that its customers know what they want – if they come to the site through Google AdWords they are already searching for a pair of shoes. So it entices them with special offers and a call to action such as 'Sale' or 'Buy Now'. Its basic rule is that all ads must lead to a page with the product on it, because shoe shoppers will leave if they don't immediately see what they are searching for. It has found that it is the small improvements that make the difference, and its sales are growing.

Schuh has worked with Google UK to try to come up with easier ways of helping customers. It aims for what the Google website calls 'conversion'. Google describes conversion as something that 'occurs when a user completes an action on your site that you consider to be valuable. This can be making a purchase, downloading a file or requesting additional information'. Conversions can be seasonal in the shoe business – for example, not many people hunt for boots in the summer, or sandals in the winter. Schuh use the analytics Insights for Search seasonal trends button with a wide date range (for example '2005 – now') to see when search volume is highest so it can discover, for example, that its Christmas best-selling items are Ugg boots and trainers.

Google has a Conversion Optimiser that allows Schuh to specify a maximum cost-per-acquisition (CPA) bid. This is the most it wants to pay for each shoe sale from its site. Using information from the site the Conversion Optimiser then predicts in real time which clicks are most likely to result in a conversion. Based on these predictions, the Conversion Optimiser sets higher CPA bids for more valuable clicks and lower CPA bids for less valuable ones. Schuh worked out the maximum amount that it wanted to spend on each sale or lead before advertising costs mean that it wouldn't be making a decent profit. The amount changed from product to product – expensive leather boots had a higher CPA than plastic flip-flops. Sometimes it increases the CPA to see if that will lead to more sales of the expensive boots that have a bigger profit margin than the cheaper flip-flops. What is interesting is that the Schuh team are keeping an eagle eye on what is selling and why.

Schuh is always updating and improving the website and has used the Website Optimiser tool to test which pages of its site work best. For example, it wanted to know if customers bought shoes when shown a big picture or if they were happy with smaller pictures. So, it created alternative versions of the test page, one with a big picture and one with a small picture. The Website Optimiser showed each of the alternative versions to different visitors. The two different page variations took the shopper to the checkout where they could buy the shoes, and Schuh found out which picture was more successful.

If you place the analytics tool on the key pages of the website it will start tracking all the people that visit the website and it can start telling you information about:

- what country they come from;
- sometimes what county or city they come from;
- how long they stay on the website;
- whether they just saw one page and went away or whether they came and saw lots of pages.

If you get more in-depth information, you can tie the analytics to actual purchases and it can tell you how much people are spending, the value of the things that people are purchasing and what pages they see before they purchase. It can inform you how big the screen is that the people are surfing the internet on, so you can tell whether you need to make your web page work well on a small screen or whether it's ok to make it fill up the whole of a big screen. It can also tell you whether people are on dial-up modems or broadband connections.

Analytics can also give you a lot of information about how the different keywords perform; much of this information is in the basic AdWords feedback, but Analytics has the deeper and better interface for looking at how certain keywords perform over time, whether they got people to just come and look or whether they actually turned it into purchasing. It's a very powerful tool.

Activate for Analytics

(This should take 30 minutes.)

1   Go to the Reports tab in your AdWords account and it will take you through the steps for setting it up; the basic steps are adding a little piece of code to your website.

2   Download the code. Add the code to your web pages and... that's all there is to it. If you put the code in your header and footer of the web pages, then it will appear on every page of the website. Once that code is on your website all the tracking will start to happen and it will flow back to your Analytics account immediately.

3   The results will be shown to you in a panel, a dashboard, which shows you how your traffic has done over the last few days. It has a graph that shows you whether your traffic's high or low. It shows you where your traffic is coming from on a map of the world and you can drill in and get more detail on any of these areas.

Traffic sources

Analytics can tell you whether people are finding your website direct – and direct means that somebody is typing in your website because they've heard of you – or whether they're coming from search engines. If they're coming from search engines, it shows if they are coming from Yahoo! or Google and whether they are paid or non-paid. (So far we've been talking about paid AdWords traffic, but there's also non-paid. If you come up in the free results, it's called 'organic' and can be significant.) If you drill down even further, it'll start to tell you what words people are typing in to find you, which is very helpful in figuring out which AdWords work best for your business.

ACTION POINTS

- Don't start making decisions on things with too little information.

- There is interesting information coming in to Analytics every day (depending upon how big your website is and how much traffic there is) and it may be information you can act on.

- Don't rush to change things until you can see a pattern.

CHAPTER 4

Managing success

This final chapter is about the upside of running your own business, and how to manage the business so that you make money as well as having fun. I will show you the steps to:

- finding investors;
- growing the business;
- building a following through blogs;
- how to sell your business once you are successful.

Finding investors

Let's be realistic here. I'm guessing that you are broke and have invested all your spare cash and all your time and energy into your new business. You are probably working in your chaotic office dressed in a scruffy T-shirt and you don't go out much because you are running an online business. *You have to change.*

The first major task is to step back from your business and think about its potential. You are going to need facts and figures. You are going to have to write a business plan that can attract investors. The business plan will include:

- a description of your idea;

- how much money the business will need to expand;

- a SWOT analysis (strengths, weaknesses, opportunities and threats);

- a set of accounts, preferably signed off by your accountant.

There are many good templates for writing business plans, but don't expect this to be a speedy process. You need to create an honest picture of your business, but of course you also need to show all the great advantages you bring.

The second task is to consider who you would like to invest in your business. At this stage you are probably just thinking about the money! Many small businesses start with investment from their family – but do you really want to risk your mother's pension? This is the moment when you need to decide who would be the perfect investor. If your business is 'Mum's cookies' then yes, your mother would be just right. But maybe you need an 'business angel' with other skills. An 'angel' is often an entrepreneur who has made his or her millions and now wants to invest in a business at an early stage. Angel investors often have specialist knowledge and invest their time as well as their money. There are a few questions you need to consider as you need to know who you are looking for:

- How much money do you need?

- How long will the investor want to work with you?
  (Many expect to sell within three to five years.)

- Do they bring other expertise to your business;
  do they have experience in your field?

- What percentage of the business will the investor want?

Most angels want to find a business with growth potential that will give them high returns for their risk. Many work in syndicates so you will have several investors. Often they want to find a business that is geographically close to them, so it makes sense to start looking for investors close to home. You will discover that investors like to be recommended to the start-up company; they are not enthusiastic about cold callers. So you are going to need to network to find your angel:

- Attend the trade organization for your type of business.

- Go to business seminars and trade fairs (**http://www.biztradeshows.com/** has lists of different trade shows in different continents).

- Join community organizations – the city trade and commerce groups.

- Network with as many people as possible.

When you meet likely investors you need to have your business plan available for them to examine. There are several online websites that will host your plan for investors to look at; they usually ask for a monthly fee. See, for example, **http://www.vfinance.com/**, **www.angelinvestmentnetwork.co.uk/** and **http://www.businesspartners.com/**.

ACTION POINTS

- Create a SWOT analysis (strengths, weaknesses, opportunities and threats).

- Prepare a set of accounts, preferably signed off by your accountant.

- Use your networking skills.

Growing the business through a blog

Why do you want to blog? According to the *New York Times*, 95 per cent of blogs are dropped and forgotten within three months of starting. Before you start, ensure you have the time and commitment to continue.

You are the only person who can answer the 'Why do I want to blog' question honestly. The best answer is that you have something useful to tell people and that your blogging will create global interest in your business or service. For example, if you have a holiday rentals business you might want to blog about great holiday destinations, but then you need to ask yourself – who is going to read this, what do they want to know? What expertise can I bring them?

Perhaps the purpose of your blog is to attract people to your website from a particular locality – maybe you have a cake shop in the west of your town, and would like to attract customers from a wider radius, so you will be blogging to attract the cake buyers from the south. You might focus on writing about celebrations, such as children's birthday parties and how your cakes are perfect for children. Although you are aiming for parents with children in the south of your town, you might find that there are many more parents with children interested in your views on birthday celebrations. After all, your blog is live 24/7 and there are interested parents all over the world. You have an opportunity to make money as well as marketing your business.

AdSense

This is where you might begin to create an extra revenue stream: you can place your blog on AdSense and make money from it.

Google AdSense is a Google program based on content rather than on search. Both blog and website owners who sign up for AdSense can display Google ads on their content and receive money for any clicks on the ads.

CASE STUDY
Rock Jock making money out of content

Geoff runs a gay-themed fitness site called Rock Jock. It contains fitness tips and information about fitness programmes with a slant to the gay/lesbian community. AdSense runs alongside the information.

So, if you're selling Lycra clothing to people who like to exercise in comfortable, figure-hugging clothing and have set up your AdWords ad to show on the content network, your ad will appear on the Rock Jock pages if Google thinks it is relevant to Rock Jock's content. Every time a visitor to the Rock Jock site clicks on your ad, Google will charge you a fee and 50 per cent of that fee will go to Rock Jock because it created the attractive content.

Content owners who sign up for AdSense can display Google ads on their blogs websites and receive money for any clicks on the ads. Google uses a web crawler, Mediabot, to crawl web pages to analyse content. It then places ads that specifically relate to the content onto those pages. Google's content network has become the largest network of advertising sites in the world. When you sign up for AdWords, if you tick the box saying 'show this on the content network' the same ad will automatically go out on the content network.

This means that your ad will appear on websites within the network that discuss related topics. Your potential customers may not be actively searching for the service you offer, but now, while they browse this website, they are faced with your ad. Effectively, you are placing a link to your services right in front of the very people most likely to want to hire you or buy from you – those that are already interested in or are researching the subject you have products to sell around.

ACTION POINTS

- Pick a name for your blog that includes the name of the product or service you are selling.

- Be conservative about how much time you have.

- You can register your name and domain name for very little outlay – but your expertise and your time are expensive.

- Write for the people who you want to bring to your website or who will want to buy your services.

- Keep your content searchable in Google so that a high ranking in the search engines creates new visitors for your blog.

- You can make money through cost per click with programs such as AdSense – you receive money for every click on your blog.

The beauty of an online business is that start-up costs need not be enormous, and the internet offers the chance to grow the business as big as you like, or to stay small and select if you prefer.

Fortune favours the bold, however, and as well as drawing together the threads of the lessons you'll have learnt so far, our final chapter is about the very real rewards that online selling can bring. It features the inspiring story of a man who was disillusioned with his corporate career. He took the brave step of resigning to start his own business, and eventually became a multimillionaire through a simple but clever online sales proposition. It didn't happen overnight, but through good times and bad he never lost faith in his idea, and in the end it paid off, many times over. In this case study you'll discover:

- how a niche proposition can become enormously profitable;

- why getting in early on a new idea is both a blessing and a curse;

- how almost every disadvantage can be turned into an advantage;

- how to start local but finish global; and

- how to make your business so successful and attractive that your competitors want to buy you out!

CASE STUDY
Richard Coundly and his holiday rental site

In the early 1990s, Richard Coundly was a tired and frustrated man. He had been working for one of the UK's biggest corporations in a high-powered job that reported directly to the company's Treasurer. Unfortunately, Richard and his boss did not always see eye to eye, and it had been a relief when he had been asked to step out of his position for a while and take on a new project working directly for the Chief Executive, redesigning the structure of the company.

The project was a roaring success. The Board loved the restructure plan; Richard and the rest of the team were told their work had been 'exceptional'. The *Financial Times* ran a double-page spread on the restructuring, and the company's share price leapt. But when it came to his annual appraisal that year, to his amazement Richard's old boss denied him any bonus at all, marking him down for not having achieved his objectives in his old job, even though the reason was that he'd been seconded to the restructuring project for most of the year. The blatant unfairness of it rankled. Richard knew he could never again be happy in the corporate world. He hated the politics, he realized he despised many of the people he worked with, and felt like, as he puts it, 'a square peg in a round hole'.

Meanwhile, he and his wife had recently invested in a holiday apartment in Ireland. 'We'd been staying with friends, and my wife was really keen to own one of these new apartments that were being built. It was her idea, not mine, but I wanted to keep her happy, so we used some savings, borrowed from her parents, and somehow scraped the money together.'

Their plan was to let the apartment for some of the year, to cover their costs, but when they advertised the apartment in *The Times* in the UK, there was little response. It started Richard wondering about how other people with similar lets advertised their properties, and since he and his wife had been thinking about setting up a small business of their own, after his disappointment in the corporate world, he began making plans for a listing service for holiday property owners.

'All we wanted to do in the short to medium term was to create a business that would pay the bills,' says Richard. 'Initially we were thinking of a paper-based brochure or magazine – in other words, doing exactly what was already being done by other companies – which would have been an uphill task against established competition. But this was 1995, and I was becoming fascinated by the possibilities of the internet. I'd watched everything at work being networked, and realized that once you start on that road, you never go back – it changes everything. It dawned on me online was going to be a great medium for advertising holiday lettings.'

When he and his wife analysed the potential of their business idea, they realized they could be onto even more of a winner than they'd thought. There was no need to restrict the business to advertising only Irish holiday lettings, or even lettings in the UK. Yet the existing business base was surprisingly fragmented even at national level, let alone an international one. 'I could see there was a longer-term opportunity to consolidate. You could use the internet to build a business that would dominate the whole market and be global in scope.'

Richard's was a simple but brilliant idea. With a paper listings business, you are held back by the physical size of the product. No one wants a great thick telephone directory of a brochure to drop through their letterbox – even assuming it would fit! 'But with an online listings business, our inventory was infinite in size. We could sell space to people with holiday property all over the world, and offer holidaymakers a choice hundreds of thousands of apartments and cottages.'

Richard and his wife took the plunge in 1996 and set up one of the very first online holiday property listings sites. He sold space on the site for people to advertise their holiday properties for let. Revenue would be generated by charging a fixed fee – annual or six-monthly – to the property owner.

'There are both advantages and disadvantages of being early in the field,' he says. 'Yes, you're getting in first, and you're not running against entrenched competition. But the disadvantage is that it can take an awful long time to get things going to a scale that generates profit. You are launching in a new area, using new and untried technology.'

When their listings service launched, it had just 15 properties on its books. 'It doesn't sound much, does it? But that's another way in which online scores over any other way of doing business. If you were publishing a holiday property magazine, it wouldn't be viable. But online you can afford to start small and add to your inventory incrementally, because once you've spent the money to get the website up and running, the costs of adding another property, and then another, and then more, are actually quite low.'

But it wasn't enough, as we have already learnt, simply to put up a website and hope people stumbled across it. Somehow Richard had to market the site. And these were such early days for online businesses that nobody really knew how it could be done. 'Again, that's both a disadvantage and an advantage,' he says. 'You don't know anything, but neither do your competitors know anything about how to market online. The big corporates were slow off the mark. The successful guy is the one who learns fastest – the good problem-solver, if you like.'

Richard, with a degree in engineering and an MBA from the London Business School, had a background in problem-solving. Nonetheless, the first few years were hard. Holiday property letting was seen as a niche within the wider travel market, so it was impossible for him to win any venture capital – investors at the time were too busy looking for mainstream opportunities. So it took faith, and staying power, through the lean years.

But sometimes, Richard says, it actually helps that you don't have much money. 'For a start, there won't be too much competition in the field, because no one else can raise capital either. And if you're strapped for cash, there is only one way to survive: to be smart. The well-financed start-ups were lazy. They had the money to go to advertising agencies, and they just blew it – handed the agencies half a million quid for campaigns that didn't work. We had to look for other ways of marketing ourselves – and that was when I made the big discovery that it was the search process itself that was the key to success online.'

Richard knew he had to market his business to two different groups: those who owned holiday property, and those who wanted to rent it. 'Back in 1996 it wasn't at all clear how you would reach online customers – whether it would be through traditional routes like newspaper and TV advertising, or using directories or some kind of internet portal. The breakthrough idea came when I went to talk to potential customers and discovered that everyone wanted their search to be simple – to type what they needed into a box and hit "find". They wanted to use search engines. Today it seems obvious, but search companies like Google and Yahoo! were in their infancy then. It hit me that the way to online business success had to be some kind of search engine optimization, and we put all our energies into finding ways to make our website rise high on the list of results that appeared when someone typed "holiday let" into their search engine.'

Richard understood what many others in the field did not at the time, and so became one of the first to realize the potential of exploiting search engine technology to grow his business. By using techniques like Google AdWords, he gained an advantage over the competition, and then the business really began to gather momentum. The more people came to his site to look for a holiday let, the more holiday rental property owners were attracted to buy space on it. Now money was starting to flow in as the business achieved critical mass.

'If you look at any listing business, you'll realize that size matters. There are economies of scale, which are critical to profitability. Your unit costs go down, your profitability goes up. But there is also what I call "competitive advantage of scope". In other words, if you attract someone to your website, you want to maximize the potential for them to actually find what they want, by having as broad a selection on the site as possible. Once an online business gets past the tipping point, all it ever does is spew money back at you as you grow to dominate the marketplace and dominate the search engines.'

All the long hours Richard and his wife had put into the business were at last paying off. By now others were copying what he had done, and 'me too' holiday let sites were springing up online. But Richard had been first and fastest. He had also gained an advantage over the competition by developing a completely integrated web-based platform to run the whole business, handling subscriptions, marketing and even the bookkeeping. As a result, others came to him to buy or rent the same technology for their sites, and now he was also making money as an applications service provider. Indeed, the enterprise was so successful that Richard eventually pulled off the coup that everyone in business envies – having made his fortune from selling, he then made even more money by selling the company!

'Right from the start, I had believed there was an opportunity to consolidate the holiday lettings business on a global basis. A company in Austin, Texas, called Home Away, had similar ambitions, and they had raised the venture capital to snap up competitors in the States. But they lacked the technology platform that we owned. Once they realized how successful it had made us, they decided they needed to cross the Atlantic and buy us out. To use the old cliché, they came up with an offer we simply couldn't refuse.'

Richard became a multimillionaire overnight. Better still, because he believed in Home Away's global strategy, he was canny enough to take a third of the payment in shares as well as retaining a seat on the board. As a result he has made money over and over again since the sale of the company he started. He has his own private plane, an enviable lifestyle, and the satisfaction of having achieved his dream.

Remember:

- If you're strapped for cash, there is only one way to survive: to be smart.
- Economies of scale are critical to profitability.
- As your unit costs go down, your profitability goes up.
- Ensure your technology platform is robust for expansion.

How to sell your business once you are successful

Richard's story is an inspiring one. But what lessons could you take from it?

First, don't be afraid to start small. At the same time as the internet offers all the scope of an enormous inventory, it also allows you to launch with a tiny one, as Richard found. You can take your time to build the business as you discover what people are most interested in buying from you, and although it is worth doing some market research first, once you are certain that there is a market for what you want to sell, be it a physical commodity, or ideas, or information, or listings, don't delay. Once you have a good idea of how your site should look and have the money to build it, go ahead. Although the initial outlay might seem steep, remember that unlike a paper-based business, the cost of adding items to your inventory will be minimal.

Second, find your niche. When Richard started his business, nobody was prepared to invest in what seemed only a tiny part of the wider travel business. But he proved them wrong, by growing a niche enterprise into a potentially global one. If you can find the right niche, there may well be opportunities of consolidating once the business starts to grow.

Being early in the field can be a massive advantage. That isn't to say that a 'me too' company will fail, but you will have to work harder and be even more clever to find that competitive edge if there are already many others preceding you in the same market. On the other hand, the early starters will have made all the expensive mistakes, so you can learn from their experience, but to beat them you will need to find a twist that makes your business stand out.

Don't let lack of investment deter you. As Richard discovered, being short of cash can make you more creative than the opposition. Be prepared to think outside the box, and you may latch onto the next Big Idea.

Times may well be hard in those early months. You will very probably have to work long hours, and as Richard found, it will feel as if you are pouring money into a bottomless pit. 'All we ever seemed to do was stick money into the business, with nothing coming out: investing, investing, investing.' What kept him going? 'Just a refusal to give up, really. Keeping faith in your idea is essential.'

Once the business takes off, make sure you keep growing your inventory to take advantage, as Richard did, of that 'competitive advantage of scope'. You want to be sure that your website becomes known as the one where people will find what they are looking for in your market – just as eBay or Amazon have done in the wider marketplace. Being competitive in price is helpful, but remember the lesson Richard learnt from his early meetings with potential customers – online, people like the search process to be simple and may go no further than the site that carries the bigger range. Again, it's all about reputation – this time not just for the quality of the service you offer, but the scope of your inventory. You need to be competitive on price, service and *choice*.

Be creative in the way you approach technology. What made Richard's business so attractive to others in the long run was its technology platform. If you can develop one that is superior to any of your competitors', they will want to join you, and you can generate income from selling or leasing your technology to others.

Finally, don't be afraid to think big. Richard freely admits that though he was looking for a way of paying the bills at the start, he was also bold enough to think ahead to the long term and spot the possibilities for growing his business globally – another advantage of selling online.

So what advice does he have for people thinking of starting an online sales enterprise? 'Someone once asked me *how* I became an entrepreneur,' says Richard. 'But "how" is easy – you just start a business. Anyone can do it. The real question is "why". If the answer is that you really want to run a business, you hunger to try out ideas, to be your own boss, to let the marketplace judge your performance rather than the HR department, to follow your dream, go ahead and do it. You'll never look back.'

ACTION POINTS

- Start small, but think big.

- Look for a niche that no one else has yet begun to exploit.

- Don't let lack of investment hold you back – think of creative solutions to marketing problems.

▶ Keep the faith in your dream, and don't give up too soon.

▶ Expand your inventory to dominate the market.

▶ Reputation, as always online, is key. You need to become known not only for good prices and great service, but also for a wide range so people know they will find what they want on your site.

▶ Look for ways of being creative with technology, so you can sell your business solutions to others.

▶ Sell up when you've exhausted the possibilities of getting more enjoyment from your business, and enjoy the proceeds of your labours!

Conclusion

There are as many different ways of making money online as there are people who want to get rich. You will need more than the advice in this book – you will need to work hard, be innovative and... get lucky. Having spoken to all the individuals in the case studies contained here, it is clear that they have one key characteristic in common. They are passionate about what they do. So my best advice to you, my reader, is to create a business that you love, that gives you satisfaction. Then you will have a deep understanding of your customers and provide them with the goods and services that they most need. In these ideas lie success and a business that you enjoy.

APPENDIX

Ensuring your personal privacy

While you are building publicity for your business, you might also have concerns about how to ensure your online privacy.

Although it is almost impossible not to have an online presence in the 21st century, not everyone welcomes it. What one person sees as making their mark on the world, another may see as bordering on personal intrusion.

Today's culture is very different from the one previous generations grew up in. This is an era where celebrities happily share their heart-break, their 'drug-hell' weaknesses, their sexual ambiguity and their children's illnesses. People routinely share information our grand-parents' generation would have blanched at. Being 'open' is seen as a virtue. Being 'discreet' is felt by some people these days to be even a little dishonest.

If you are writing a blog for your business you will be aiming to create interest in the products you are selling or the ideas behind your consultancy. It is easy to be carried away by the confess-all culture into thinking that everything should be shared. However, although allowing an online presence to reveal your humanity may often be desirable, and can help promote your business, it is also worth remembering that discretion has its good points too. Our grandparents had a phrase for it: don't wash your dirty linen in public. By which they didn't just mean the downright grubby. They also believed there was very little value in washing even the 'once-worn' under other people's gaze.

This appendix covers what can be done to maintain your personal boundaries online. It will look at why some people might want to have a lower profile online, and how that can be achieved.

To begin, a short personality test:

1   The doorbell rings. A glance through the peephole reveals a neighbour on the doorstep, holding a parcel she has taken in on your behalf. Do you:

   A. Ignore the bell and pretend you are not in?

   B. Invite her in for a cup of coffee or glass of wine?

   C. Thank her, take the parcel, and close the door?

2   On a long train journey, the man in the opposite seat makes a remark that could be the prelude to a conversation. Do you:

   A. Bury your head in your book/newspaper/laptop?

   B. Launch immediately into conversation and by the end of the train journey have shown him photos of the kids/the dog/ your nearest and dearest you keep on your phone?

   C. Respond politely but allow the conversation to peter out.

3 How many of your workmates have been to your home?

   A. None?

   B. Most of them – you love opening your home to hold parties even for people you don't know well?

   C. One or two, with whom you have struck up a friendship.

Those who tend to answer A are intensely private people, maybe bordering on anti-social. Those who go for Bs are on the whole eager puppies in their relationships, friendly, trusting and outgoing. Those who go for Cs are more cautious, willing to be friendly but setting clear boundaries.

While on one level this is no more than a bit of fun, it might be worthwhile taking a moment to consider the implications of your personality type when it comes to deciding how much of yourself you should reveal on your website, not to mention on sites such as LinkedIn and Twitter, which may also be used to promote your business. More and more, it has become customary to post personal information online. With the rise of Facebook and other social networking sites people are encouraged to share their circumstances and experiences with others, in an open way. There has been much discussion in the media about safety for children online, but remarkably little consideration of what adults should do to safeguard themselves and the reputation of their businesses in this relatively new environment.

How the online environment is different

It is worth remembering that the online environment can be very different from the real world.

The stranger on the train to whom you show your family photographs will probably have forgotten them, and most of the conversation, an hour after you have alighted at your separate destinations. He certainly will not have access to your mobile to call the pictures up again, nor will others apart from your immediate neighbours on the train have eavesdropped on the interchange.

But on the internet, what is posted for others to see may stay there for a very long time. It can easily be transferred to other people, and the person who posted it will not be aware when online pictures or the information are accessed or passed on. What is shared on the internet has a long shelf-life, and it is important to consider that when deciding what to reveal of yourself online.

CASE STUDY
Dulce Merritt, Psychotherapist Barbican Counselling

This is a case study about a business woman who, for professional reasons, does not want a personal online presence. She is managing her online image so that she is only found through professional websites, rather than on social networking sites.

Dulce Merritt is a psychodynamic psychotherapist working in Central London where she runs a counselling practice with four colleagues. Psychoherapists work from different traditions, for example the 'humanist' tradition is an interactive method of working that can allow varying degrees of self disclosure. Psychotherapists working within a psychodynamic or psychoanalytic tradition, like Dulce, have a long established process of working where they find value in presenting more of a 'blank canvas' to their clients. So, Dulce's consulting room at Barbican Counselling is plain – it contains books, paintings, a desk and phone, but no photographs. Dulce ensures that the furnishings and setting remain constant. This constancy and the lack of the personal are not accidental, but consistent and appropriate with the professional practice of psychotherapy. The practice has an online presence through its website **www.barbicancounselling.co.uk**, but the site contains only brief professional qualifications about the individual psychotherapists. Again this is part of Barbican Counselling's carefully considered communications strategy built on the needs of their professional lives.

Dulce explains 'Some psychotherapists go to considerable lengths to make their canvas incredibly blank. They don't even smile. I personally feel that can come across as cold and maybe even punitive. Every practitioner has to find the balance between being themself, their personality, and an appropriate professional stance.' For Barbican Counselling this means not disclosing personal information. There are sound reasons behind this approach, which can be understood by exploring and valuing what Dulce describes as 'the productive working creative space between the client or patient and the practitioner'. She explains that revealing personal information to the client or patient would be an imposition. This is because psychodynamic psychotherapists allow their clients to use the space as a resource and to fill it with their own thoughts and feelings. In practical terms this also means engaging with the imaginative ideas and questions about the practitioner that are in the mind of the client. The psychotherapist's training gives them the expertise to work with these fantasies and ideas and through them to explore the inner thoughts of the client.

'It's because something has gone wrong for them that they have come to talk to me in the first place, and this is one way into their internal world. It reveals how they then structure their existence and how their personality works in interaction with their life. They can't have a completely free fantasy if they know facts about me. And the fantasy is important. You could think of it rather like a dream or a feeling about an event in their life.'

So, the blank canvas is an important element of the work Dulce does with her clients. However, like all modern businesses, Barbican Counselling needs an online presence. When looking for counsellor or psychotherapist, location is an important deciding factor – in London the user will Google 'counselling in London' or 'counselling in the Barbican'. The web is an important tool for the practice and their Barbican Counselling website will appear in postcode searches and geographic searches. But the website has to avoid the personal. Dulce explains this was not an easy task: 'A website presents a visual image, in a visual medium, but we decided not to have photographs of ourselves. We worked with a designer who is also married to a psychotherapist, and understood our needs. So our site gives a sense of place with photographs taken around its location in London and also conveys a feel for what we do. In addition to descriptions of our approach and practical information, there is a picture of water, which is the Barbican lake, but also represents the unconscious, and there is a picture of the statue of the dolphins from the Barbican – dolphins represent both happiness and communication in a rather mysterious way.'

Just as the website was the product of considerable planning and care, Dulce has also ensured that any other online information is within her control. Her family would like her to have a Facebook entry (her sister uses Facebook to talk to her children who are at university; two brothers have Facebook accounts and post photographs of their families). They have asked Dulce to join them but she has demurred. Her concern is that a new client would be likely to research her background online, and could have access to personal family material and to her family links, which would not be appropriate for her professional work.

'I need to protect my identity, which would be more difficult to control were I on Facebook, even if I restricted access to my page. Photographs could be tagged, for instance. Clients come to see a counsellor or psychotherapist and they care a lot about their own anonymity. You are protecting that as well as offering, through yourself and the work you will do with them, the chance to discover themselves in a new way. They need to be able to model in their mind what they require, and not have to deal with too much of their therapist's personality. Plus, how might they feel about their counsellor's capacity for confidentiality if they also know she is posting personal items on the internet for all to see?'

Dulce's rejection of an online presence is not something she has done without thought and discussion within her practice. She points out that there are a number of famous psychotherapists who have much more of a public persona: many have published academic papers or give lectures. She cites Mike Brearley – the former Chair of the External Relations

Co-ordinating Committee of the British Psychoanalytic Society – as an example of a psychoanalyst who is well established in her field of work. As former captain of the English cricket team, Mike Brearley uses the fact that he is well known as a tool to explain his thinking. Having captained the England cricket team in 31 of his 39 Test matches, winning 17 and losing only four he writes and talks on the Art of Captaincy. Her view is that, 'You do not have to be totally secretive or anonymous but you just have to be appropriate; the work I do involves thinking about boundaries.'

Online boundaries are an area that she hears about it in her consulting room. 'I had a client who told me a Facebook story about updating the status with 'Hi I'm available tonight what's happening' and zillions of people responded to her and it suddenly hit her that it didn't feel comfortable.' Dulce's view is that the public/private space is not clearly defined online – people know the online world is public but they still paradoxically insist it has to be private as well. 'I think there is a kind of blindness. It's as if they are wanting to walk naked in the high street and then they are surprised that people are shocked.'

Dulce thinks that the individual should consider more carefully where to draw the line and create boundaries between public and private. Here Dulce recognizes what she calls 'collective learning' in today's teenage generation with a different level of openness in society. But she warns that as situations change in life there are some areas that would be better to remain private – the errors of youth are not appropriate information for business clients: 'I did things when I was a teenager that I would not want people to know about now – everybody does! I didn't rob any banks but I did stuff like all kids do.' Her conclusion is that just as clients in her counselling practice come to discuss issues of boundaries, so the younger age groups will need to learn online image control and understand the boundaries between public and private.

Online safety tips for adults

It is not difficult to understand why home addresses, telephone numbers and so on should not be published online. But people should also be wary of posting photographs that inadvertently reveal where someone lives. If a house is in any way unique, it can be recognized, especially in conjunction with other information, such as the general area in which someone lives. Consider, when posting photographs not only of your own home, but those of friends, that other information may be freely available elsewhere online that would enable someone not only to pinpoint an address, but to combine that with information about a person's movements. Even an innocuous caption to a holiday photo such as 'The family relaxing at our timeshare villa in Italy last July' may have given away more than intended. A would-be burglar might take a guess that since the family were at the timeshare last July, the chances are they will be there again in July this year.

Identify the information you are prepared to allow online

Equally, apparently harmless information released in a personal blog or an 'events' or 'news' column on a website should be carefully weighed to be certain it will not cause problems by revealing too much. An author who posts details on their website of their personal appearances, for instance, is revealing when they will be away from home. In itself, this is not an issue, but they should remember that other information elsewhere on the internet could have rendered them more vulnerable than they realize. It is not so much what is revealed in one place, but what the implications are of that information being taken in conjunction with other freely available personal data, that has to be thought through. It is not difficult, for instance, to find an individual using websites such as 192.com, which combine information from electoral rolls, telephone directories, and other sources. A determined journalist has always been able to track down an address, but now the kind of resources that were once the province only of professionals are available through the internet to everybody.

Pride in one's achievements, coupled with the desire to seem friendly and approachable, has been the downfall of more than one person online. A year or two ago, the about-to-be head of Britain's Secret Intelligence Service MI6, Sir John Sawers, received a great deal of unwelcome publicity when it was revealed that his wife had posted family photographs on the social networking site Facebook. The then British Foreign Secretary denied that security had been compromised, pointing out that the fact Sir John wore Speedo swimming trunks was hardly a state secret. But Lady Sawers had failed to activate privacy controls on her Facebook entry, and had thereby revealed the location of the family's London flat, as well as the whereabouts of the couple's three grown-up children and Sir John's parents.

A foolish mistake can result in the collapse of your reputation and your career hopes. In the United Kingdom a prospective Conservative candidate for a local council in Kent resigned after a poor judgement with his use of Facebook. Payam Tamiz, was due to stand for election to Thanet District Council but had joined a group that referred to local women as 'sluts'. He apologized 'unreservedly' for any offence, but his reputation was tarnished and career as a politician has suffered a set-back. Here the key message is:

Don't join Facebook groups, or any other groups that will tarnish your reputation.

Even if you have not made a foolish mistake, it is important to manage your business and your personal material in a consistent form. For example, in Stoke there is a charming and old-fashioned real estate agency that has a website offering services that are 'professional, respectable, and reliable'. All well and good. But if you Google the name of the company owner his Facebook site shows his mains hobbies are dancing at raves and paragliding. These are fine and fun activities, but not aligned to reliability. Here the key message is:

> If your hobbies and your professional career are separate, ensure that your hobbies are online under a different name – perhaps you might use your first name or your nickname followed by the hobby – so your Facebook page might become Dave-the-Rave, rather than David and the name of your business.

If you are considering your online reputation you need to understand the effects of search engines on your business. The world's largest independent PR agency, Edelman, which has over 3,700 people in 53 offices worldwide, provides research about the issue of trust in business. In 2011 it investigated how people find information about companies and discovered that the first place that people go to find out about a company is a search engine, with an online news source as the second place and print coming third. In simple terms, what they discovered is what we all know: if you want to find some information about a business you 'google' the name of the company.

So it is crucial that what is said about your company online, and appears in the first page of the search engine response, is both accurate and creates a great impression of your business activities.

Youthful looking Jon Ferry created a reputation problem for himself in search engines when he was interviewed about his marketing company by a national newspaper. The interview was a successful promotion for his business, but it created a difficulty in the search engine result. The journalist accurately reported his age, which is 65, a perfectly good age, but not something that Jon promoted to his clients. Jon is a marketing expert for new technology and many of his clients are in their late 20's and early 30's and he did not want them to treat him as a grandfather! If a search engine was used to find out more about Jon's marketing skills, one of the first stories found is the one from the national newspaper, and its headline reads 'Jon Ferry, 65, has a marketing success with new technology'. Jon does not lie about his age, but equally he doesn't want it brought to the attention of all his clients. So what can he do? The key message is that good news drives out bad news, so Jon now needs to create more stories about his company and his youthful activities that will balance the one story that contains his age.

The nuts and bolts of successful gate-keeping

Those and similar horror stories circulating about the perils of posting online might deter many people from having any sort of online presence. However, it would be foolish to cut oneself off completely from the advantages of being there. Successful gate-keeping is all about being aware of the global scope of the internet, and the potential permanency of anything posted there. Understanding the internet's public nature, and not expecting privacy as a default setting, will help people only add to their online profile the kind of data they are prepared to share with all and sundry.

Think before you post

The secret is to think before you post. Every time you plan to add a picture to your site, or sit down to compose your personal blog, ask yourself whether you would be prepared to share this thought with your worst enemy, or that picture with the creepiest person you know. Double-check privacy controls, if you are using a social-networking site, and be prepared for their failure.

Unless you are entirely happy to bare all online, it is wise to think of your online persona as needing to be guarded by a series of protective filters. In other words, it is sensible to grade information about yourself so that you have a clear idea of what is to be shared by immediate family and close friends, what might be seen by a wider circle of acquaintances, possibly including clients and business associates, and what is to be available to everybody, including total strangers.

Know your boundaries

It is vital to know yourself well enough to set your own personal boundaries. As Dulce Merritt points out, 'You do not have to be totally secretive or anonymous but you should be appropriate.' That could mean thinking through how posting anything personal could impact on your professional life. It might seem amusing to post a set of photographs of your (or someone else's) misspent youth – the school football team mooning from the coach windows on a trip to an away match – but consider how your (or their) clients will react to it. Would you really want to take the risk of alienating people who might not share your relaxed attitude or your sense of humour?

As a starter, sit down and compose a list of what information you are prepared to share with the world. Ask yourself next:

- What impact sharing that information will have on your professional life and your business.

- Will it enhance the way clients/customers see you, as a friendly human face in an impersonal online world of commerce?

- Do you feel it could adversely affect your relationships with clients?

- Will clients respect you more or less if they are able to access your holiday snaps online?

The answers to those questions will depend upon the nature of your business. However, they also depend on your own individual nature: how private or how public you are prepared to be – and it is wise to know yourself before allowing other people to know everything about you.

Closing the door after the horse has bolted: can anything be done to take down damaging or inaccurate information on the internet?

It is relatively easy to police your own postings. But a large part of the information that exists on the web about individuals is not necessarily posted by themselves. People should be alert as to how they are portrayed, not only on their own website or social networking site, but also to entries posted online by other people.

Sharing photos is common on social networking sites, and sometimes, though embarrassment is not necessarily intended, moments better forgotten can re-surface. A minor embarrassment or two is probably no bad thing for the soul, as an antidote to hubris, but occasionally there may be good reasons why a seemingly innocent snapshot should not appear – for a person in a similar role to Dulce's, for instance, who wishes to preserve their anonymity for professional reasons. It might not be a photo – sometimes old friends decide to reminisce about the past's wilder moments, adding such unhelpful information as '... and old Johnners, who was the instigator of the whole affair and personally draped the lady's underwear over the statue of the founder, is now a High Court judge!'

If the offending item has been posted by a good friend or relation, the obvious remedy is to contact them and ask them to take it down. The friendship may suffer as a result, and you may go down in their estimation as a kill-joy, but it might be worth it if you have genuine reason to believe your business or professional reputation will suffer, or if personal information is revealed that might put someone at risk. If you approach them politely, explaining why you are concerned and asking them to imagine themselves in your position, they will probably accede to your request if it is a reasonable one.

It goes without saying that the same understanding is unlikely to be accorded to the famous. Celebrities have to learn to live with embarrassing moments surfacing from their past. Indeed it is more likely that a celebrity who complains will only receive more unwelcome attention, and be pilloried for having no sense of humour. In such cases it is probably better to grit your teeth and ignore the offending picture or anecdote.

But what if the item is not merely professionally embarrassing but also untrue? There are several notorious incidents involving the online encyclopaedia, Wikipedia. In late 2005, the 78-year-old former editor of *The Tennessean* newspaper in the United States, John Seigenthaler, was surprised to discover that not only was he apparently a suspect in the assassinations of both John and Robert Kennedy, he had also lived (without noticing it) in the Soviet Union for 13 years. The information had been posted in his Wikipedia biography as a prank – but it had been online for four months before he knew about it.

The strength of Wikipedia – that it can be edited by anyone – is also its weakness. Since Mr Seigenthaler wrote about his experience in *USA Today*, Wikipedia has been more vigilant, and maliciously false information is often taken down within hours of posting, or even within minutes on more high-profile entries. Nevertheless, info-vandals are everywhere online, and it is possible for misinformation about an individual to find its way onto the internet and take root.

This is especially worrying if the information is on Wikipedia, as its entries tend to score relatively highly on search engines, so anyone searching your name via Google, Yahoo or other engines will come across it sooner rather than later. Much of the time its 'mistakes' are a source of mirth and fool no one but the most gullible – the film actress Deborah Kerr, for instance, was reported to have retired from the screen to found a chain of abattoirs. But occasionally misinformation appears that could seriously damage a person's reputation or affect his or her professional life. Politicians tend to complain most loudly about this, although there is evidence to suggest that some of them are not above tampering with Wiki entries themselves.

The Wikipedia entries for some politicians, including Barack Obama, enjoy special 'semi-protected' status so that they cannot be modified by anonymous users. Nevertheless, British politicians David Cameron and Nick Clegg were not accorded that status in the year before they formed the Coalition Government, and during that time visitors to their entries could have come across the untrue claims that that Mr Cameron's father had 'bought' him the leadership of the Conservative Party, and that Mr Clegg had slept with 3,000 women and become a member of a hip-hop collective called the Wu Tang Clan.

It is not so difficult to spot that such claims are false, and they were taken down very quickly by Wikipedia's team of volunteer administrators. However, another British politician, Liberal democrat MP Martin Horwood, found that his entry had been altered in such a way, he believed, as to affect his chances of re-election in a key marginal seat. His immediate impulse was to try and correct the entry himself, but he was warned that this was considered bad form by the administrators and that any changes he made would be removed. It took a great deal of negotiation, and some back-up from technologically literate friends, to arrive at a form of words that the administrators were prepared to allow to correct the perceived bias.

What can be done about online misinformation, be it malicious or an innocent mistake? In the case of Wikipedia entries, the person (or company) that is the subject of the article is not allowed to edit it. Nor is it always a good idea to ask someone else to do it for you. Some years ago, a Microsoft employee objected to what he thought was 'slanted' language in a Wikipedia article on a Microsoft project. Recognizing that it might not look good if Microsoft applied pressure to Wikipedia for the article to be changed, he e-mailed a contact outside the company and asked him if he would be prepared to look at the article and correct it so that it was more objective. But the idea backfired when the contact went public, implying that Microsoft had been trying to use him to manipulate their image.

A better solution is to raise the issue in Wikipedia's own discussion area. If the information about you or your company is demonstrably inaccurate, contact Wikipedia and ask them to take it down. Meanwhile, start an online conversation anywhere you can about what has happened, in order to spread the word that you have been the victim of misrepresentation.

It is of course necessary to have discovered the misrepresentation in the first place. Googling oneself is usually seen as vanity. Perhaps it should be seen instead as an essential form of vigilance, in an online world where reputations can be made and lost in an instant.

Action to stay in control

📇 Know yourself.

📇 Follow the questionnaire at the start of this appendix.

📇 Ask yourself the following questions:

- What impact will sharing that information have on your professional life and your business?

- Will it enhance the way clients/customers see you, as a friendly human face in an impersonal online world of commerce?

- Do you feel it could adversely affect your relationships with clients?

- Will clients respect you more or less if they are able to access your holiday snaps online?